THE
WILD-BIRD
CHILD

A life of Amy Carmichael

DERICK BINGHAM

AMBASSADOR

BELFAST, NORTHERN IRELAND
GREENVILLE, SOUTH CAROLINA

The Wild-Bird Child
© Copyright 2003 Derick Bingham

ISBN 1   84030   144 9

Published by the Ambassador Group
Ambassador Publications
a division of
Ambassador Productions Ltd.
Providence House
Ardenlee Street,
Belfast,
BT6 8QJ
Northern Ireland
www.ambassador-productions.com
&
Ambassador Emerald International
427 Wade Hampton Blvd.
Greenville
SC 29609, USA
www.emeraldhouse.com

———•◦•———

To Dr. James C. Barton,
who led me to Christ;
and who has devoted his inspiring life
to the people of India.

———•◦•———

A little wild-bird child,
But lately caught, and nowise tame,
And all unreconciled
To cages and to careful bars
That seemed to ban the very stars.

———•·•———

From the autobiographical poem *Sweetness Wherever*
by Amy Carmichael.

CONTENTS

ACKNOWLEDGEMENTS

The author wishes to thank the staff of the *Public Record Office of Northern Ireland* for their most generous assistance as he researched this biography. Around two hundred letters, forty-one volumes, and two files, relating principally to the life and work of Amy Carmichael, have been placed there by *The Dohnavur Fellowship* and Miss Margaret Wilkinson, under the designation D/4060.

He also wishes to thank *The Dohnavur Fellowship* for their more than kind permission to quote freely from this unique and inspiring archive: he is deeply grateful for the help and guidance given by Jean van der Flier, Margaret Wilkinson and Dr. Nancy Robins.

The poetry of Amy Carmichael quoted in this biography is from the superbly edited book, *Mountain Breezes: The Collected Poems of Amy Carmichael*, <u>CLC</u>, Fort Washington, Pennsylvania, 1999. It is used by kind permission, and is an intregal part of this work. The storyline of this biography and some quotations are taken from the landmark biography, *Amy Carmichael of Dohnavur* by Frank L. Houghton, © 1953, The Dohnavur Fellowship, published by <u>CLC Publications</u>, USA. Used by kind permission.

Factual material about the present day work of *The Dohnavur Fellowship* and some quotations are taken from the video, *Amma: The story of Amy Carmichael and The Dohnavur Fellowship.* Used by kind permission. This excellent 52-minute video is distributed by Evangelical Films, Danbury Common Old Mission, The Common, Danbury, Chelmsford, Essex, CM3 4EE, England.

The author also wishes to record his profound thanks to Mrs. Dorothy Finn for typing the manuscript of this book over a period of six months. She did this work with verve, enthusiasm and constant cheerfulness. Above all, as a deeply committed church member on Belfast's Shankill Road, Dorothy displayed a great empathy towards the subject of this book, who served God so faithfully in the Shankill area before moving to service overseas.

Illustrations

Inside illustrations by Kerrie A. Bingham.

Kerrie A. Bingham is an Honours Graduate in Visual
Communication from the University of Ulster. She is currently
working as a Graphic Designer.

"But first learn to pronounce us. Doh rhymes with so, go, lo. Ur rhymes with pure, sure, lure.

It is not Donnva. It is Doh na vur. Ur is the same word as Ur of the Chaldees, and means village, town. Dohna is the name of a German Count who founded the place a hundred years ago. V is to join the vowels.

Now, then, say it, please – Dohnavur.

That Dohnavur is heaven, is a mistake that a good many make. After the squabbles of the villages, and the dust and disorder and noise, the quiet order and the beauty of green trees and flowers, and above all the happiness of the children, impress most who come into it in much the same way. They turn to one who is showing them round and say, 'It is heaven.' They little know the battlefield it is, for that does not show on the surface, nor does one wish that it should. Then, too, the way by which the needs are provided, as they say, 'by the hand of God,' impresses the intelligent very much. They are all in debt, and when they hear there is no debt here, they stare all round astonished, and count up the cost of the nurseries, and the immense quantity of rice required per day. Sometimes they say slowly to themselves, 'Then God knows when the bills come in and He sends the money beforehand to be ready' (which is surely the literal fact). When they see us doing without anything, as they do if they are long enough with us, they are puzzled; for the idea of test of faith, or of discipline of faith, is, of course, far out of their sight; but they do see that we are content to do without, and something at least of the meaning of peace dawns upon them."

Amy Carmichael
Dohnavur Letter
June 1924

PREFACE

IT WAS a beautiful March afternoon, and I was walking past College Gardens in Belfast with my friend, Os Guinness. He had just spoken at the Queen's University Christian Union, on the subject of Evil and Suffering in Our World, and his unique gift as a Christian apologist had soared. As we walked, we got talking about Amy Carmichael, who in her youth had lived at No. 21, where Os's great grandfather, Grattan Guinness, used to visit. Grattan, the grandson of the Dublin brewer, Arthur Guinness, had been right at the heart of the great spiritual awakening in Ireland in 1859, when around 100,000 people came to personal faith in Christ in one year. In fact, the largest buildings for his use failed to accommodate the numbers who thronged to hear him.

Os's aunt, Joy, had been a friend of Amy Carmichael, and they had corresponded for years. Joy had passionately longed to write a biography of Amy; but, due to her commitment to caring for Os's grandmother, she was unable to do so. Joy lived and died in Sweden. As we continued walking, Os suddenly began to vigorously challenge me to show in this biography that Amy was not just a great missionary, but that she was also a great social reformer. I use the word 'challenged' in its fullest sense, for my friend had a look in his eye that said, "If you don't, then you are not being true to her legacy to the world."

When I was in the Northern Ireland Public Record Office on Balmoral Avenue, Belfast, doing some research on the village of Millisle in County Down as it had been in 1867 when Amy was born, I 'stumbled' on the original letters of Amy Carmichael. They had been placed there by *The Dohnavur Fellowship* and Miss Margaret Wilkinson. In reading those letters I found spiritual gold. I came to love that distinctive handwriting, chronicling the ways of God in the nitty-gritty of Amy's life; and I felt my heart being drawn out after her Lord, in a deep, refreshing way. I often sat with those letters in my hand, surrounded by thirty-three-and-a-half miles of public records, and worshipped God.

It did not take long to find out that my friend Os was right. When, in some temples, Amy discovered a custom of the time, where children were 'married to the gods' and introduced to a life of cult prostitution, she set herself to discover the full facts in order to compel the Government to act. I shall never forget coming on the line in one of her letters: "I have begun this because I want your prayers. *The subject is National not just Missionary in its bearings.*" So, the social reformer was on her way.

As I write, on my desk lie novels written by Indian authors, describing India in all of its democratic chaos, anguish and greatness. Here, too, is the tangle and perfume of India. A while back I got some audiotapes of Rudyard Kipling's incredible *Kim* (how I love to have somebody read to me!), and was intrigued by the India that he unravels. E. M. Forster's *A passage to India* is, in his own words, "about the universe as embodied in the Indian earth and the Indian sky."[1]

But Amy Carmichael's India is different to these. She sees and writes about it through very different eyes: eyes touched by the salve that gives double sight (see *Revelation* 3:18).

Once, when I was teaching the Scriptures in Geneva, Switzerland, I was taken one afternoon to visit a chalet outside the city, where I was introduced to a retired missionary. When the lady heard that I was from Northern Ireland, she immediately asked me if I knew of Amy Carmichael. Well, of course I did – Amy's story and her writing have long been a deep source of Christian influence on my life. The lady then explained to me that, when she was much younger, she had worked in Dohnavur, during the time when Amy was an invalid. One day Amy said to her, "I will light a light in my window at night. That light is for you." As the tired, sleepy young missionary headed for her bed after a busy day, that light became a deep encouragement to her.

Amy shone a light for more than that young missionary – she has lit a light for millions, which beams on us even in the twenty-first century. It emanates from the One who is the Light of the World and the Light of Life; that is, the One who gives us enough light to live in.

Dr. Os Guinness has pointed out, "In an age that endlessly celebrates celebrity and shamelessly consumes the lives of the rich and famous, it is salutary to remember the ancient Jewish and Christian axiom: many of the greatest heroes are unknown and unsung, unaware of their own significance."

He points out that such people, "of whom we know nothing, have arrested cities and nations from disaster in an hour of peril. Doubtless, others have been solitary sentries at the frontiers of a menaced family or community. Perhaps only for their sake were such things as justice, sanity, beauty, humanness and freedom of worship not taken away when forfeited earlier – as in the story of Sodom and Gomorrah, destroyed for the lack of ten good people.

"Most heroes, however, cannot remain unknown. They need to be known to be emulated. Thus, not even disgust over hollow celebrities must deprive us of genuine heroes who can fire our imagination, stretch our hearts and minds in an effort to mimic their lives and hold out for us models into which we can pour our searching aspirations. In short, heroes help us grow further and higher than we ever could without them."[2]

I have sought to make this hero a little better known, particularly through her letters. That she was a hero is irrefutable; what she did and said has led multitudes to righteousness, and to worship God.

Here, then, is an attempt to uncover the heart and mind of the hugely self-effacing 'Wild-bird child' from Millisle, who, by God's grace, soared. By that same grace, may the life of Amy Carmichael truly inspire us to stretch further and higher.

Derick Bingham
Belfast
Summer of 2003

1

It Did Not Make Her Brown
Eyes Blue

IT WAS 1867. Queen Victoria, known as 'Her Britannic Majesty', was 48 years of age. She was declared to be, "By the Grace of God, of the United Kingdom of Great Britain and Ireland and of the British Dominions beyond the Seas, Queen, Defender of the Faith." Despite their unsurpassed Empire, the British were still an insular people. A Victorian headline read, "FOG IN THE CHANNEL, CONTINENT CUT OFF."

Class distinction was rife. On Sundays, the week-enders would gather in the chapels, found in every great country-house, and sing:

The rich man in his castle,
The poor man at his gate:
God made them high and lowly,
And orders their estate.

This attitude could be seen in a small but significant detail of Victorian life: if a member of the House of Lords was sentenced to the gallows, he was hanged with a silken rope.

It was the year in which Johann Strauss II composed *The Blue Danube* waltz, John Galsworthy and Marie Curie were born, and a truly great man died. Somehow, through his life and work, he had broken through the rigid class system of his age, and had transcended all classes. Born the son of a blacksmith, he became a chemist and physicist, and is arguably the greatest scientist England has ever known. Called the 'early morning light' of electrical science, and later acknowledged as the 'father of electrical engineering', the results of his discoveries unquestionably inaugurated our modern industrial, commercial, and social world. Once when he was lecturing in London, he held his audience enthralled for an hour as he demonstrated the nature and properties of the magnet. As he closed his lecture his audience burst into applause, and the Prince of Wales rose to propose a motion of congratulation. With huge applause it was immediately seconded and carried. The audience waited for his reply, but the lecturer had gone. Where could he be? He had gone to the prayer meeting of a little church where he was an elder – a church that never boasted of more than twenty members. He never neglected the weeknight prayer meeting. He had slipped away from the applause to renew fellowship with God.

He was offered, but he refused, the Presidency of the Royal Society. He was twice offered, but he refused, the Presidency of the Royal Institution. He was offered, and again he refused, a knighthood, commenting, "I must remain plain Michael Faraday to the very last." He did, however, accept a 'grace and favour' house on Hampton Court Green, awarded by Queen Victoria.

As Michael Faraday lay dying, they tried to interview him. "What are your speculations?" they inquired. "Speculations? I have none! I am resting on certainties," he replied. "I know whom I have believed, and am persuaded that He is able to keep that which I have committed unto Him against that day!"

Faraday made a statement that has since become famous: "*The book of nature, which we have to read, is written by the finger of God.*" No one was to believe that truth more than the little girl born on December 16th 1867 to David and Catherine Carmichael in the Irish village of Millisle, County Down. She would later write in a thousand ways of the discernible finger of God in nature. Amy Beatrice Carmichael was to revel in seeing the spiritual in the natural.

With Elizabeth Barrett Browning, she would believe that 'earth is crammed with Heaven.'

And no wonder. The island on which she was born has a beauty all of its own; in particular, the fertile plains of the northern half of the Kingdom of Down have proved to be immensely attractive to centuries of settlers. Generations of British fleets, which helped to create the Empire, were built from the oak forests that covered these plains until three hundred years ago. Cleared of the forest, the land was planted with crops and fruit trees, and covered with herds of sheep and dairy cattle, thus creating the basis of one of the strongest agricultural industries in Europe. Today, the nearby Strangford Lough (Gaelic for lake, or sea), an inlet with seventy islands, is home for up to twelve thousand Brent geese in summer and autumn, before they return to the Arctic in winter. Wintering dunlins top 20,000 in number, and if you could count oystercatchers, curlews and other waders together, you would reach the 100,000 mark. In her childhood along the coast of County Down, Amy would have seen redshanks, ringed plover, Iceland gulls, and breeding cormorants.

The growing Amy Carmichael fearlessly rode her pony up and down the long beach at Millisle, where mustard coloured lichens roughened the black stones, and butterfish wriggled. Once thrown, when riding on the main road, she lay stunned by the sea wall, and had to stay in bed for weeks. But soon she was back in the saddle, riding full tilt into the wind, the salt spray in her hair and face and her heart thumping. Whenever her pony, called Fanny, was frightened, she did startling things; but Amy discovered that if she sang softly into her ear it soothed her. Amy was not averse to spirited escapades, such as once climbing out of the skylight in the bathroom of her family home and triumphantly leading her two little brothers round the roof along the lead gutter. Gazing down, she discovered her parents watching, and it was not one of her happiest moments, when she had to crawl through the skylight into their waiting arms.

David Carmichael taught his children to swim by fastening a belt around them, one by one, with a rope attached. He would then throw them into the deep water of the dam. He loved to take them for walks and he and his wife made their lives as interesting as possible.

The eldest of seven children, Amy quite often visited her grandmother at Portaferry on the beautiful Strangford Lough, where her uncle was a local doctor, as her grandfather had been before him. The Vikings, who were present in the area from 800-1000 AD, had named the Lough 'Strangford,' meaning 'violent fjord.' This refers to 'The Narrows' which runs between the villages of Strangford and Portaferry at the southern entrance to the Lough. It takes approximately 350,000,000 cubic meters (or tonnes) of water to fill the Lough from low water to high water. All this water can only get into the Lough by passing through The Narrows. Hence a vast river of water rushes through The Narrows at speed of up to 7.5 knots. The tide takes six hours to come in, and six to go out. The tides are said to be the second strongest in the world. During the ebb tide, at the bar mouth entrance to The Narrows, a heavy breaking sea can be encountered. This is particularly dangerous, with any form of wind from the south to east creating a swell. Breaking seas of up to 8 meters have been seen. Add to this the local 'Routen Wheel,' a large circulating eddy, characterised by whirlpools caused by a ledge of rock only 4.6 meters below the surface, and it will be understood that The Narrows area is not a safe place for children to row. (The name 'Routen Wheel' was given by the Vikings, as they thought the sound of it was like cattle snoring!)

Within limits, the Carmichael children were allowed to go out rowing; but one evening they passed those limits, and were caught in the current that swept them towards the bar mouth of Strangford Lough. Amy was steering and, though rowing hard, her young brothers were powerless against the fast-moving current. "Sing!" they shouted to Amy – though only God knows why. So she sang the first thing that came into her head:

He leadeth me, O blessed thought,
O words with heavenly comfort fraught:
Whate'er I do, where'er I be,
Still 'tis God's hand that leadeth me!

J. H. Gilmore

Fortunately the local coastguards heard Amy's song and rowed to their rescue before the children were swept over the bar. The finger of God in nature, and the hand of God in intervention, were themes that lay close to Amy's heart through all of her life. At times she would lie beside the rock pools on the beach at Millisle, and with intense fascination gaze into the life within them. Later in her life she wrote:

Our love is like a little pool;
Thy love is like the sea.
O beautiful, O wonderful,
How noble love can be.

So the sea kept surfacing in Amy's poetry: the coast of the Ards Peninsula where she lived as a little girl had left indelible impressions, long remembered even after enduring decades of the searing hot seasons of South India. In one of her poems of worship she wrote:

God of the deeps, how near Thou art;
Here are Thy garments: sea and shore.
Beauty of all things show in part
Thee whom, unseen, we love, adore.
Thine are the good salt winds that blow;
Thine is the magic of the sea;
Glories of colour from Thee flow –
We worship Thee, we worship Thee.

God of the tempest and the calm,
God of the tireless, patient tides,

God of the waters' healing balm,
And gentle sounds where stillness bides.
God of the stainless fields of blue,
God of the grandeur of the sea,
Swifter than ever spindrift flew,
Like homing birds, we fly to thee.
God of the waves that roll and swell,
And break in tossing clouds of foam.
Thy handiwork, the painted shell –
For fragile life, how safe a home.
God of the great, and of the small,
God of the glory of the sea,
Here, in the quiet evenfall,
We worship Thee, we worship Thee.

The Industrial Revolution of the 18th and 19th centuries had left its mark on the County of Amy's birth. The rushing waters of streams and rivers were harnessed to power the hundreds of linen mills which sprang up around the countryside. A hundred years before her birth, Amy's great-grandfather leased the two flour mills which dominated the village of Millisle, and her father and her Uncle William developed them. They were powered by a little stream, dammed up to form a lake in the middle of which was an islet. According to the locals, it was this islet that gave Millisle its name. For this author, though, the village will be famous for one incident above all others. With a passion, Amy was determined that God would change the colour of her eyes from brown to blue. Blue was her favourite colour; and it is not without significance that most of her books were to be bound in blue cloth. Let her poetry tell the story:

Just a tiny little child,
Three years old,
And a mother with heart
All of gold.

Often did that mother say,
"Jesus hears us when we pray,
For He's never far away;
And He always answers."

Now, that tiny little child
Had brown eyes;
And she wanted blue instead,
Like blue skies.
For her mother's eyes were blue,
Like forget-me-nots. She knew
All her mother said was true –
Jesus always answered.

So she prayed for two blue eyes,
Said "Good night,"
Went to sleep in deep content
And delight.
Woke up early, climbed a chair
By a mirror. Where, O where
Could the blue eyes be? Not there!
Jesus hadn't answered.

Hadn't answered her at all!
Never more
Could she pray – her eyes were brown
As before.
Did a little soft wind blow?
Came a whisper, soft and low,
"Jesus answered. He said 'NO.'
Isn't 'No' an answer?"

During the Second World War a Jewish rescue farm was set up near Millisle. Children will know about it through the famous award-winning novel by Mandy Taylor, *Faraway Home*. Those brown eyes of Amy Carmichael were to be one of her most useful attributes, when she would be led to rescue hundreds of brown-eyed children from unspeakable things, and establish a faraway home for them. God was about to take Amy away from her first home. Never again was she to live by the Irish Sea, but her love for it and its place in her heart were to remain with her forever.

A Wild-Bird Child

2   IT WAS 1879. Albert Einstein and Joseph Stalin were born, and Emmeline Pankhurst, the Suffragette leader, got married. Britain had just recently finished the construction of one maritime and two overland telegraph links to India, on the back of Alexander Graham Bell's recent invention of the telephone. London got its first telephone exchange, and the Tay Bridge collapsed in Scotland. The great engineers, Stephenson, Brunel, Locke and Vignoles had built their railway lines across hills and mountains, valleys and marshlands, rivers and valleys. Railway stations had brought a new type of building into British culture; and all of this was now being extended throughout the Empire. In 1879, the dining car was first introduced to railways; and, in the midst of all these rapid changes in communication and transport, Amy Beatrice Carmichael made her way to Yorkshire. She was only twelve.

Educated in Millisle by a succession of governesses, particularly the dearly-loved Eleanor Milne, Amy now found herself at Marlborough House, a Wesleyan Methodist boarding school in Harrogate. She was not the first Irish girl to go to Yorkshire. Before her, the immortal and gifted Bronte sisters had gone to Haworth from the same Irish County. One wonders if Emily, Charlotte or

Anne were ever as homesick as Amy, who wrote that she was:

> A little wild-bird child,
> But lately caught, and nowise tame,
> And all unreconciled
> To cages and to careful bars
> That seemed to ban the very stars.

Amy decided to defy the bars, and headed for the stars. One evening in 1882, a comet was to appear in the night sky. The girls in Amy's dormitory asked her to request permission from the Principal of the school, Miss Kay, to allow them to sit up and watch the comet. When Amy duly asked, she was told in no uncertain terms that permission would not be granted. That night in the dormitory Amy tied threads to the large toes of her compatriots, and held the ends of the threads, promising to keep awake until everyone in the house was asleep. At the right moment, the fourteen-year-old Amy pulled the threads, and softly up the creaking staircase the schoolgirls proceeded, nearer and nearer to the stars. The attic window and the flaming stars beckoned, as the comet hurtled towards their vision. But what was this? As they stepped towards the window in the dark, shadowy figures suddenly rose up before them. The school Principal and the entire teaching staff of Marlborough House were watching for the comet. Amy shuddered, her blood pressure surged, as one overwhelming thought emerged: "Is this it? Will I be expelled?" In such school regimes in Victorian days, it was a distinct possibility. Nowadays, the entire school would probably be watching for the comet, equipped with the latest telescopes and digital cameras; while most of their teachers might be asleep!

As it turned out, Amy and the rest of the girls from her dormitory were allowed to stay and view the comet. In the morning, Amy was given an hour's 'ticking off ', but she did not have to suffer the indignity of expulsion. One suspects that the 'wild-bird child' got into many confrontations with the 'cages and bars' of her boarding school education. Later, in a family magazine, she wrote ironically about what happened *When the Teacher Left the Room*:

Girls were more like a pack of boys
Than like the gentle girls
I've sometimes called our pearls
Of innocence and peace
And quiet loveliness.

She describes how there was much 'Clatter, chatter, hurry and rush', and particularly a rushing for the blackboard, when the teacher slipped out of the classroom for a little while. She names some of the girls she knew as 'Maud Davison,' 'Ethel Scuttleback,' 'Eva Lamefoot,' and 'Louise Onionsleek.' One can imagine their escapades, and they certainly don't sound like stuffed shirts. Amy undoubtedly had a streak of the rebel in her. Later, though, she stated that she regretted many things that happened which should not have happened, because she had not learned to set to and work at things that seemed dull and not useful. To be fair to the school, Amy is on record as saying that there was not a teacher whom she didn't love.

At this point in this autobiography my spirit can empathise with Amy. Likewise wild, and certainly untamed, I too came under the influence of one of the greatest Christian organizations for children in Britain. As I look back on my childhood, I would acknowledge that its red and white banner truly stands out as a guide to what my life has been about. It is the C.S.S.M. By God's touch, gently and powerfully it has been many a child's handmaid for the Christian cause. To many generations of boys and girls, the Children's Special Service Mission has given free access to intriguing fun-filled days, and the careful presentation of Christian truth. Multitudes of people have grown up appreciating its admirable work.

It was near the end of Amy's years at Marlborough House that the C.S.S.M. held a Mission in Harrogate. They could not have realised the full repercussions of their well-intentioned work. The gospel seed they sowed was to have an Indian harvest. By God's grace that little team of Christian workers in Harrogate were to touch Amy Carmichael's heart and life, and through her the lives of children in South India, who otherwise would have been the victims of a horrendous trade. The speaker at one of the C.S.S.M services at Harrogate, Mr Edwin Arrowsmith, asked the children to sing the words of the famous hymn *Jesus loves me, this I know*, and then to be quiet for a few moments. In those quiet moments, that immeasurable love drew Amy into the safekeeping of Christ's fold. The Good Shepherd, who gave His life for His sheep, had called Amy to Himself. Right to the end of her influential life she was to come to know His voice intimately, and follow Him closely. She put it this way:

It is not far to go,
For Thou art near.
It is not far to go,
For Thou art here.
And not by travelling, Lord,
Men come to Thee;
But by the way of love,
And we love Thee.

Back in Ireland, things were changing on the County Down coast. There had often been changes. In 432 AD Saint Patrick was brought by God's guidance to the area. He had meant to sail up the coast to County Antrim, but strong currents swept his boat through Strangford's tidal narrows. So he landed in County Down, where he spent the next thirty years preaching the gospel to the Irish, dying at Saul in 461 AD. The Vikings, the Normans, and later, at the Plantation of Ulster, the Scots, all sailed to the County Down coast. In fact, the Carmichael family had come from Ayrshire. On Amy's father's side, they were of Scottish Covenanting stock. The first in the family to settle in Ireland was James Carmichael, who was born in 1705, and is buried with his sons in Bangor Abbey churchyard. Amy's mother was Catherine Jane Filson, who was a descendant of the Dalziels of Scotland, who were friendly with certain persecutors of the Covenanters. Amy found significance in the fact that it was love that eventually brought the persecuted and persecutor together.

From the sixteenth to the nineteenth century, the nearby port of Donaghadee was the most popular route into Ireland from Scotland. The little port saw many famous people pass through its harbour, including Peter the

Great – the Tsar of Russia, and the greatest of all English Romantic poets, John Keats. Daniel Defoe, the author of *Robinson Crusoe*, came through Donaghadee as a spy. The Carmichaels had landed imported American wheat for their flour mills at Donaghadee; but of recent times their trade had come under pressure from imported American flour. So they decided to move from the County Down coast to Belfast, and build a new mill at Dufferin Dock. David Carmichael's family moved to 21 College Gardens in the south of the city. As financial restraint began to bite into the family's resources, Amy was brought home from Harrogate, and her brothers from King William's College on the Isle of Man. For Amy it served to great advantage, for it meant she had a closer relationship with her father.

David Carmichael was a man of real literary taste. He studied Classics at what is now known as the Royal Belfast Academical Institution, in preparation for University education. But David decided not to go to University, entering the family business instead. He was an innovator, not only at the flourmills, but also in introducing and rearing improved breeds of cattle. He adopted the principles of Land Reform, long before they were widely accepted and eventually legalized under William Gladstone's leadership. In politics David was active in the Liberal Party, helping to establish the Ulster Reform Club; and he was equally energetic in supporting free trade. As a Justice of the Peace, he took part in public discussions on the disestablishment of the Irish Church. He had raised his family in the Ballycopeland Presbyterian Church, where he taught Sunday School. When the minister, Rev. John Beatty, was unwell, David sometimes took the Sunday evening evangelistic service in the Millisle schoolhouse, where he would often read one of C. H. Spurgeon's pithy and spiritually nourishing sermons. In David Carmichael's time, Spurgeon was arguably the greatest preacher in an age of preachers, and his sermons were published every week. His sixty-three volumes of sermons now stand as the largest set of books by a single author in the history of Christianity.

Spurgeon had two horses that were widely regarded as the best in London. The Archbishop of Canterbury used to borrow them for State and Royal occasions. On a Sunday, they drew Spurgeon in his coach to the Metropolitan Tabernacle, where thousands gathered to hear him preach. When someone criticised him for working his horses on a Sunday, Spurgeon replied with characteristic humour, "My horses are Jews, and always rest on Saturdays!" On January 8th 1882, Prime Minister William Gladstone attended the evening service at the Metropolitan Tabernacle to hear Spurgeon preach. David Carmichael was a supporter of William Gladstone, but Queen Victoria could not endure her Prime Minister. She famously commented that he addressed her like a public meeting, ". . . that mischievous firebrand; arrogant, tyrannical, and obstinate . . . a half-crazy, and in many ways ridiculous, wild and incomprehensible, old fanatic." On a trip to London, as Amy and her father sat watching Gladstone in the gallery of the House of Commons, one is certain that Victoria's view was not shared by the Carmichaels!

Amy was now eighteen, and a dark shadow fell across her vibrant and wonderfully creative life. Through sheer benevolence and Christian kindness, her father had lent some money to a friend in need. When the time came to pay back the money, the friend was unable to do so. David Carmichael would not take the man to court or force him in any way to pay back his debt. Other losses began to impinge on David's business life and, weakened by the pressure, his health became vulnerable to infection. In the early part of a week, he caught a severe chill; and on the following Sunday morning, April 12th 1885, while the church bells were ringing, David Carmichael died of double pneumonia. He was fifty-four.

Amy became a second mother to her family. In life she carried one great characteristic, namely empathy: she had an outstanding capacity for putting herself into the shoes of anyone who was in trouble. In one significant moment, that facility was to change the entire direction of her life. Indeed, she traced the unique work to which she was eventually called to an incident in the year of her father's death, on the way home from the Presbyterian Church in Belfast where the family worshipped. On that dull, wet, grey, Belfast morning they met an old woman dressed in rags, carrying a heavy bundle. Moved by pity, Amy and her brothers turned round, relieved her of her bundle, and, taking her by the arms, helped her along the street. The little group was now pushing against the throng of surprised, 'respectable' people heading in the opposite direction. It was certainly going against the tide of respectability. Later Amy explained that they had hated doing so, and were deeply embarrassed. Just as they passed a recently built fountain (it is generally accepted that this is the fountain still to be found outside the British Broadcasting Corporation's premises on Ormeau Avenue), some phrases from Scripture came into her mind and seemed to speak into the grey drizzle of that morning:

Now if anyone builds on this foundation with gold, silver, precious stones, wood, hay, straw, each one's work will become clear; for the Day will declare it, because it will be revealed by fire; and the fire will test each one's work, of what sort it is. If anyone's work, which he has built on it, endures, he will receive a reward. If anyone's work is burned, he will suffer loss; but he himself will be saved, yet as through fire. 1 Corinthians 3:12-14.

Amy turned to find where the voice came from, but there was no visible person. It was still a dull, grey, Belfast morning, but she always maintained that something happened in that moment which permanently changed life's values for her – it was her defining moment. The only things that could ever matter again would be eternal things.

If it was a tide of Victorian respectability that she ruffled that morning in Belfast, it was nothing to the tide she would ruffle in coming days in South India. This wild-bird child would soar for God like an eagle; she would run and not be weary, walk and not faint. And, even in the twenty-first century, we would rise up and call her blessed.

Swinging Off The Rafters

3   IT WAS 1886. Frances Hodgson Burnett published her novel *Little Lord Fauntleroy*, and the Hungarian composer and pianist, Franz Liszt, died. Millais painted his famous child portrait *Bubbles*, which the manufacturers of Pear's soap were especially fond of using. It is hard to believe that their advertising copy contained the following words:

The first step towards lightening
The White Man's Burden
is through teaching the virtues of cleanliness.
Pears' Soap
is a potent factor in brightening the dark corners of the earth
as civilization advances,
while amongst the cultures of all nations
it holds the highest place – it is the ideal toilet soap.

In the history of cleanliness, 1886 was a vital year: Ernst von Bergmann began to sterilise surgical instruments for the first time. In Canada, the mighty waters of the Niagara Falls were first harnessed for hydro-electricity; and the Canadian Pacific railway was completed. In the United States, the *Statue of Liberty* was dedicated. In India, the first Indian National Congress met.

In September 1886, Amy Carmichael visited a Convention in Glasgow, held on Keswick lines. 'Keswick lines' – what does that mean? In the spiritual history of Britain, a very important event had taken place in June 1875 in the beautiful Lake District town of Keswick. In the hands of God it was destined to become one of the greatest annual Christian Conventions in the world. Its primary aim since its inception has been to present the Biblical claims of practical, personal holiness, so that Christians would be encouraged to live a life worthy of their status as the people of a loving God. The Keswick Convention and its satellite Conventions across the world have resulted in multitudes of lives being transformed by the teaching of Scripture – quite recently, I have had the privilege of speaking at all seven of the Japanese Keswick Conventions. It is a never to be forgotten the experience to sit in the great Convention tent at Skiddaw Street in Keswick at the Communion Service on a Friday night, surrounded by several thousand Christians from all over the world, beneath the Keswick Convention flag which states *All one in Christ Jesus*.

The speakers at the very first Convention in 1875 were Rev. G. N. Thornton, Rev. T. Philips, Mr. H. F. Bowker, Mr. T. M.Croome, Mr. Shipley, and a remarkable Anglican clergyman, called Prebendary William Webb-Peploe. A talented athlete, despite having suffered serious spinal injury while a student at Cambridge, and having lost an eye when scratched by a cat, he was able to play tennis into his seventies. This mercurial and distinguished man had been on holiday in Yorkshire the year before. On the fourth day his baby son died. He carried the little coffin in his arms throughout the prolonged journey home; and he buried his little one with his own hands. His text for the following Sunday was *My grace is sufficient for you; for My strength is made perfect in weakness* (2 Corinthians 12:9). Suffering the deepest grief, William threw down his pen and cried, "Lord, let Thy grace be sufficient. O Lord, do!" The word *is* in the text suddenly took on a huge significance. A voice seemed to say to him, "How dare you ask God to make what is. Get up and take, and you will find it true." That little word, *is*, transformed his entire life. For over forty years the insightful teaching and potent oratory of William Webb-Peploe was to be at the heart of the Keswick Convention, along with the voices of J. Hudson Taylor, F. B. Meyer, G. Campbell Morgan, W. Graham Scroggie, and many other eminent Christian leaders during his lifetime. His gifted grandsons were to be deeply involved in Amy Carmichael's life.

In September 1886, as Amy sat in a Glasgow hall, full of a sort of grey mist that does to this day invade buildings in that city of welcoming people, she heard the Chairman of the Convention closing a session in prayer. "Lord," he said, "We know Thou art able to keep us from falling." Amy, who admitted that her soul was in a fog at that stage in her Christian life, suddenly found the fog lifting. The words that the Chairman had used encapsulated the assurance of victory that God gave her on the path she wanted to follow as a disciple of Jesus Christ. The Lord could indeed keep her from falling, and present her faultless before the presence of His glory with exceeding joy (see Jude v.24). She need not fear to walk the path of discipleship, so it was with an added inch to her step that Amy returned to Belfast.

Amy's activities for the Lord Jesus were many. She organised children's meetings in her family home, and established what she called The Morning Watch. A group of boys and girls pledged to spend time in prayer and Bible reading each morning. They then met on Saturday mornings, and each in turn spoke of how they had got on, and what they had learned. If they had missed their Morning Watch, they admitted it. The report from one of the members was that Amy ensured there was never a dull moment. Before her life was through, this seminal trait was to touch thousands of children. 'Dull' was never a word to describe her Christian leadership.

Amy also started a weekly prayer meeting for schoolgirls, that at first was held in their own homes. Later, when some of the teaching staff and girls of Victoria College expressed a wish to join the prayer meeting, it was held on the College premises. (With three daughters of my own who went to Victoria College, I find the history of Amy Carmichael touching my life yet again!) The College was established by Dr. Margaret Byers, a former missionary to China. She believed that, under the influence of the eleventh chapter of Hebrews, one could do anything! She and Amy would have been united in such a conviction.

It was under the influence of Dr. Hugh Montgomery of the Belfast City Mission that Amy soon had her eyes opened to the wider needs of Belfast. Dr. Montgomery took Amy through the streets of the city on a Saturday evening, highlighting both the poverty and the evil. She began to teach a class of boys at night school, and was often to be found at the YMCA in the city.

In 1888 Belfast officially became a city – the largest city in Ireland. It was the American Civil War that helped to make Belfast the world centre of the linen industry. Union troops, marching through plantations, created a shortage of cotton for the factories of Manchester in England; and the favourite, nearest substitute was linen. At one stage, the President of the Belfast Chamber of Commerce estimated that 644 million miles of yarn had been spun, and that linen exports amounted to 156 million yards of cloth. He added, "This would make a girdle, three yards wide, encircling the earth at the Equator." The huge linen mills employed thousands of women, nicknamed 'The Shawlies' because they could not afford hats and covered their heads with shawls.

They became the apple of Amy Carmichael's eye. Amy and her family attended Rosemary Street Presbyterian Church, and she asked the minister, Dr. Park, for permission to hold a Shawlies' meeting every Sunday morning in the Church Hall. Courageously, he agreed. The Shawlies disturbed some of the church people, and once more Amy had to move against the tide of Victorian respectability. True to what she had learned that day when she and her brothers had helped the old lady with the bundle, Amy stayed by her calling to help those in need. Soon the church officials came to recognise her work as a very special spiritual outreach.

When the Shawlies overflowed the Church Hall, Amy looked for a new 'home' for them. In her own account of the search she stated: "We needed a hall that would seat 500; just then we saw an advertisement in *The Christian*. An iron hall could be put up for £500, and it would seat 500 people." Amy had unhappy memories of being repulsed when asked to call on people for subscriptions to a 'good cause.' When money was needed for the Lord's work she thought it much better to go directly to God and ask Him. A Miss Kate Mitchell had heard of the work for mill girls, and asked Amy to lunch in order to hear more about it. She wanted to do something in memory of a friend who had died, and so it was her choice to give the hall – she was not asked to do so. Then Amy went to the head of a large linen mill in the city, and asked for a slice of his land to rent, which she got for a nominal fee. The hall was named *The Welcome*. On opening day, Amy sat in the middle of the hall as part of the congregation. A definitive text, from Colossians 1:18, written on a long strip of wood, hung above the low platform: *That in all things He may have the preeminence*. Two of D. L. Moody's students took part in the service; and, for the first time in Belfast, the famous evangelical hymn, *I know whom I have believed*, was sung. Michael Faraday would have been delighted! Soon it echoed around Cambrai Street in the Shankill area of Belfast, where *The Welcome* stood. It became a very busy place, as Amy and her helpers reached out to be a spiritual blessing to all. From a Bible Class on a Sunday afternoon, to a Sewing Club on a Thursday night, a Girls' Meeting on a Wednesday night, a Mothers' Meeting on a Thursday afternoon, the place was buzzing.

The work of *The Welcome* continues to this day. The premises were rebuilt and re-opened in September 1959. It was under Pastor John Johnston's leadership that *The Welcome* grew from being an outreach to becoming the home of a new church, now known as *The Welcome Evangelical Church*. Its present Pastor, John Miskelly, with his wife Gwyneth, have seen the work grow to such an extent that an annex, virtually the same size as the main church building, was opened to accommodate the expanding youth work. Officially opened in September 2003, it is called *The John Johnston Memorial*.

A former pastor of *The Welcome*, Mr. Edward Young, tells me that during his time of service he spotted hooks in the rafters. Hooks? They had been attached to swings! Girls came in from their work,

(which in the linen industry would sometimes be only half-day) and played games in the hall. Their recreation would include enjoying the swings that Amy had set up for them. Maybe that's where the phrase, 'they were swinging from the rafters,' originated! I have seen the delightful photographs of the swings at Dohnavur in Amy's day, and can recognise The Shankill's contribution to the happy recreation of those Indian children.

There was another activity in which Amy was involved that, at the time, seemed to be of little significance; but this story proves the significance of the insignificant. A few years later, in 1896, a little boy was born on the other side of the Belfast, in an area called Strandtown. He became one of the greatest children's writers in the world. His name? Clive Staples Lewis. On wet, windy, Irish afternoons, as well as on sunlit days, he and his brother Warren loved to escape into a fantasyland. It was a land inhabited by animals, just as humans inhabit ours. Clive wrote the stories of Animal Land, and Warren drew the pictures. In those pre-television days, Victorian children had to create their own entertainment; and all seven Carmichael children, likewise, had very active minds.

At the Carmichael home, a very special in-house monthly magazine had been established. It contained stories, poems, sketches and jokes; as well as occasional comments on current events, the welfare of mill girls, and happenings in the life of the family. I am emphasising this magazine activity, because it would prove to be the seedbed for future, worldwide, spiritual blessing. In the magazine, all seven young people in the Carmichael home took a <u>nom de plume</u>. Amy became *Nobody*; Alfred was *SSI* (Silly Silly Idiot); Ethel was *Atom*; Eva, *Lulu*; Walter, *Blanco*; Ernest, *Oddfellow*; and Norman, *Namron*. Mrs. Carmichael was elected president, and Amy was the editor. I held some of its volumes in my hands the other day, and I honestly believe the drawings and articles would make a fascinating book. They are a mine of information regarding the sociology of the Middle Class in late Victorian Belfast. They are also a biographer's dream, because they show the stream of Amy's consciousness at this time in her life. What was the magazine called? Now there's a question! The committee who met to name it found it a difficult task. Amy stated, "It had no mother to say, it shall be so and so," and she wrote a poem about it, entitled *The Baby's Christening*:

> Committees, you will find,
> Are hard to please and changeable,
> Like the rest of human-kind.

The poem lists the various names that the family committee discussed. There was *Carmichael Chronicle*; *A Club*; *Spectator*; *Budget*; and *Gazette of the Carmichaels*. Her poem continues:

> *The Odds and Ends* was now proposed,
> And many another, too,
> Which I forged, and therefore cannot
> Tell them unto you.
> And heads were shaken, frowns were frowned,
> In efforts to declare
> A name worthy of giving
> To the infant papier.
> Then spoke a random genius:
> "We'll call it *Scraps*," quoth she.
> So *Scraps* it was, and *Scraps* it is,
> And ever more shall be.

Namron commented, prophetically, "the rest of the poets in the family are still behind the scenes; and it is doubtful where they shall appear. After such an outburst of poetical talent and genius, perhaps they had better remain where they are." So it was that, in a quiet corner of South Belfast, the buried seed of what was to become an internationally recognised poetic talent was beginning to show signs of life.

There were plenty of signs of life in the Carmichael family as a whole. In an article called *A jumble*, we learn: "Alfred and Walter fished for stickleback; Ernest's moustache is making good progress; Ethel has a cold; Alfred haircut today; Norman has ordered *Science For All* for us. *Nobody* and *Namron* have read Ruskin's *Time and Tide*, *The Eagle's Nest, Troudes Agnisdes*, and part of *The Stones of Venice* (together in the mornings). Alfred has decorated his room, with grasses and bulrushes and geranium. Ethel has succeeded in wearing her brown jacket in shower and shine. Ethel has been first in her class nearly all month. The family generally have not quarrelled more than three times a day, lately."

The joke section reveals the common trait of Irish people to poke affectionate fun at America, famous for its bigness. Such behaviour, though, has not held back a lot of them from emigrating there. Forty million people in the United States can now trace their ancestry to Ireland, and a huge proportion of them to the Province of Ulster. "Only in America," the jokes section of *Scraps* informs us, "will you find a man so tall that he is obliged to go up a ladder to shave." "Only in America do the railway trians travel so fast that the train often reaches the station considerably in front of the whistle." "It is only an American artist who can paint a snowstorm so naturally that he catches cold by sitting near it with his coat off."

Amy's formidable intellect and spirituality often surfaced in *Scraps*. The little family journal reveals the probing, penetrating, questioning, sifting mind she possessed. A work, entitled *Double-eyed Power*, by Francis Ridley Havergal, attracted Amy's attention. Such a subject was to be awesomely paramount in her life's future ministry. Her exposition of Miss Havergal's work is priceless. She comments:

"So it is in real life. We too often take what seems, as if it were what is; and all dazzled, led by flash and glitter, knowing not there is not true gold below. While, on the other hand, we conclude that, because the surface is rough and dim, the heart within is of little worth. Had we only double eyes, double-eyed power, rather, what a series of surprises an hour's work would give us."

Amy proceeds to look at people, depicting the smiling, gracious lady we envy, who is, in fact, "tired of empty glitter, yet knowing not how to get at the gold; longing for rest, yet knowing not how to find it; knowing not of higher things." She then describes the contented, humble 'shopman' who is serving the lady; who lives by the principle that he does everything "as unto the Lord, and not unto men." Outwardly, they look so different – one privileged, the other underprivileged – but the true difference is found "under the surface." In Revelation 3:18 we read of eye-salve which we can buy from the Lord, so that we might be able to truly see. Amy was beginning to 'buy' that eye-salve, and one day a nation would benefit through what she could discern.

In an edition of *Scraps* there is section which deals with the story of words – "Drifted down the ages from the far shores of long ago." It reveals Amy's fascination with words. With eyes that could really see and an inborn love of words, even in her early twenties Amy Carmichael showed clear signals of being a unique and sensitive writer. Maybe it is a blessing that she did not recognise it: some people are great, until they discover they are great.

In the April 1887 edition of *Scraps*, alongside a watercolour of mushrooms, there is a little poem by *Nobody*:

Quickly sprouting,
Dicing ever,
Now they come,
And now they go.
Pleasant to the taste, however,
As we ketchup lovers know.

So these sproutings
Of Club papers,
Growing, in a week to fade,
Still amuse us,
When their maker
Rests in old oblivion's shade.

Amy's 'sproutings' did not fade in a week; and they now do much more than 'amuse' us. Simone Weil once commented that, to be relevant, we need to say things that are eternal. Even in the fun and frolics of a little family entertainment magazine, Amy Carmichael was rooting for the eternal. There are notes that Amy put in *Scraps* on a conversation which she had with Rev. James Gallagher, author of *Primeval Man Unveiled*. Their conversation covered such subjects as the difference between soul and spirit; how far away Heaven is; and a discussion about the 'constellation of worlds.' These notes reveal a young woman who did not live merely at the level of the immediate and tangible.

In the Northern Ireland of the twenty-first century, in this year of writing, the President of the Methodist Church in Ireland is Rev. Jim Rea. He tells the story of how he once went to a meeting in the Shankill area of Belfast, not far away from *The Welcome*. An erudite speaker was giving his views on the subject of Euthanasia. On the way out, Jim Rea overheard one lady, in absolute earnest, giving her opinion on the sermon to her friend. "Look, Love," she said, "it's not the youth-in-Asia that's the problem, it's the youth-up-the-Shankill!"

The problems of the youth in Asia were soon to become Amy's problems too. The tantalising thing is that it was future editions of *Scraps* that would carry the news of some of those young people to the outside world. From the tapering, tropical half of the mighty peninsula that is India, there would come letters called *Scraps* that would influence multitudes of people. From the land of the Godavari, the Krishna, and the Kaveri, would come writing that would carry a very special light. For Amy, life would be lived in a culture of saris; not shawls. Her life would be lived out among the frangipani flowers and coconut groves of South India; not the rhododendrons of South Belfast. Rain-drenched Ireland, with its forty shades of green, would give place to a land where Alexander Frater, when faced with its shirt-drenching, pre-monsoon heat, thought that at any moment, ". . . with a whoosh and a muffled whump, the whole place would spontaneously ignite."[3] Amy's own Province, the Madras Presidency, covered 1,450,000 square miles.

But, first, came preparation; and that preparation included a slum in Manchester, and a country estate in Cumbria.

One Snowy Evening

4

IT WAS 1889. The England Cricket team was busy playing test matches in South Africa; and, in the World Series played that year between the National League and the American Association champions in baseball, the result was New York Giants (National League) 6; Brooklyn Bridegrooms (American Association) 4. The very first commercial transparent roll-film was perfected by Eastman and his research chemist, and put on the market. It was the availability of this flexible film that made possible the development of Thomas Edison's motion picture camera three years later. The top ten female names given to babies were Mary, Anna, Elizabeth, Margaret, Minnie, Bertha, Alice and Emma; Helen and Rose tied.

In the world of the Arts, the gifted Romantic poet, Robert Browning, died; and Gilbert and Sullivan's *The Gondoliers* was first performed. In May 1889, a genius and former evangelist went, at his own request, into an asylum at St. Remy near Arles in France. In the course of the year, despite poverty, recurring nervous crises and depression, he finished 150 paintings, besides drawings. He sold none that year, and only one in his lifetime; and could never have imagined the millions that would be paid for two of his 1889 paintings, *Irises* and *Starry Night*. "Colour in a picture is like enthusiasm in life," he once stated. Few paintings in history have carried more vibrant colour than *Starry Night*. It pulsates with rockets of burning yellow, amidst planets turning like cartwheels. The cosmic gold fireworks are set against a blue sky; yet, despite all the activity, the painting is strangely restful.

Van Gogh turned from evangelism because of the discouragement he received, particularly from Christians. His favourite hymn was *Tell me the old, old story of Jesus and His love*, and he had constantly been helping and evangelising amongst the poor of Belgium when the Mission he worked with turned away from him. In the same year as Van Gogh's great art was flourishing in France despite his poverty, another Christian found herself involved in evangelism in England and living in filthy conditions. Amy Carmichael, now twenty-one, had left Belfast with her mother and her sister to carry on a work of evangelism amongst factory girls at Ancoats near Manchester. At the invitation of an old friend of the family, Mr Jacob McGill of the Manchester City Mission, Mrs. Carmichael became Lady Superintendent of a Rescue Home, and Amy was living in rented accommodation close to the Mission Hall that was her evangelistic base. Her room was infested with a most memorable type of 'creepy-crawly.'

The previous year Mrs. Carmichael had called all of her seven children into the dining room of their College Gardens home. The very serious news had come, that all, or nearly all, of David Carmichael's money had been lost. Mrs. Carmichael and her family knelt around the dining room table and committed the distressing news to the Lord. During this difficult time, Amy had become a real leader in the family. She had put forward ideas and suggestions that, when acted upon, enabled their mother to keep the family together until each became self-supporting. Each of them helped to take care of their mother, and then, over the next few years, two of the older boys went to America, one to Canada, and the other to South Africa.

Amy settled in to her work at Ancoats, living in a slum and often finding it difficult to sleep at night with the penetrating yells and screams from fights in her neighbourhood. One evening Amy headed for the late train, to visit her mother's cottage in the country. She suddenly found herself mobbed by a crowd of both lads and men. As they closed in upon her, the situation became extremely threatening. Later she wrote of how, in those terrifying moments, she thought of her great-great-great uncle who had marched through a threatening crowd during some of the Irish troubles. The crowd had stood between his home in Portaferry and Strangford Lough, where a boat awaited him. The story goes that nobody dared to touch him. He got to the shore unmolested, and sailed away. So, thinking of her forebear, Amy tried to walk on peacefully. As it turned out, a woman standing at the door of her home saw Amy's distress. She ran into the middle of the crowd, grabbed Amy's hand, pulled her into the kitchen, and put a clothes-horse between Amy and the street. Whatever it was that she said to the crowd, they slunk away, from the oldest to the youngest, and Amy escaped. It would not be the only threatening mob she would face on her life's journey.

Amy was shortly to learn the lesson of a lifetime, and she put it very succinctly: "The secret of going on is getting away." She had not been giving herself enough rest or nourishing food; and the strain of overwork broke her health. Jesus called on His disciples to come apart and rest for a time; and the truth is that, if we don't come apart and rest, we will certainly come apart.

At this time, the life and witness of one of the founders of the Keswick Convention – the man who had actually chosen the motto for the Keswick Movement – became increasingly influential to Amy. His name was Robert Wilson: he was a Quaker with wide sympathies across the community, both Christian and non-Christian. He owned a Coal Mine, and had built *Broughton Grange* above the River Derwent with a spectacular view of the whole range of the mountains in the Lake District. Amy had met Robert Wilson when he was on 'Keswick duties' in Belfast; and he had become known to the family as D.O.M. – the Dear Old Man. He was actually around sixty years old at the time. His wife had died, and he had also suffered the loss of his only daughter, who was around Amy's age. He invited Amy to come and convalesce at his home in Cumbria. It was 1890, and he asked Amy's mother if she could stay with him for the greater part of the year, and be as his own daughter. Amy's mother consented. Amy affectionately called him 'Fatherlie', and, until Robert Wilson's death, she signed her name 'Amy Wilson-Carmichael'. He became an absolute anchor in her life. Coming from a land of tragic beauty, where one is seldom allowed to simply be called a Christian – a place where denominationalism is imbibed almost with the mothers' milk, Amy watched and learned from Robert Wilson the meaning of the truth of being 'one in Christ Jesus' with other believers. As a Bible Teacher at the Keswick Convention and experiencing the fellowship for myself, I can empathise with Amy.

Robert Wilson was the chairman of the Keswick Convention at this time, so Amy came in contact with a galaxy of Bible teachers and Christian leaders, including the uniquely-gifted F. B. Meyer. When Meyer preached at Keswick once on the subject of Holiness, the next day the local Post Office ran out of Postal Orders, because Christians were paying their unpaid bills! The beauty of a Church of England service, and the quietness of a Quaker service, taught Amy much; and forged in her a determination to recognise the body of Christ wherever she found it. This became a very important attitude, for in later life it helped her as she led a very special ministry to children, which necessitated working with Christians from different denominational backgrounds. *Broughton Grange* was a school of God for Amy, particularly in what she learnt from the Godly life of its owner. One feels that he perhaps became too possessive of Amy; but it worked to her advantage, for he was a wall of protection and support to her during the rest of his life. She learned to be silent regarding things she knew about other people, in sharing the letters of the Convention Chairman.

Amy also learned to live with those who did not make her welcome. Robert Wilson's two bachelor-sons, William and Gordon, found it very difficult to accept someone from outside their family circle into the routine of their lives. It called for much discipline on Amy's part; and it proved to be a good training ground for the day when some missionaries formed a committee in India, that could have been called the 'Get-Amy-Carmichael-out-of-India' committee.

Amy was to disturb a lot more people than William and Gordon Wilson. They did eventually come to appreciate her, but the tension in *Broughton Grange* cannot have been easy to handle. As Amy put it later in her poem *What is Discipline?*:

When I refuse the easy thing for love of my dear Lord,
And when I choose the hardest thing for love of my dear Lord,
And do not make a fuss or speak a grumbling word:
That is discipline.

When everything seems going wrong and yet I will not grouse,
When it is hot, and I am tired, and yet I will not grouse,
But sing a song and do my work, and yet I will not grouse,
But sing a song and do my work in school and in the house:
That is discipline.

When Satan whispers 'Scamp your work,' –
To say to him, "I won't."
When Satan whispers 'Slack a bit,' – to say to him, "I won't."
To rule myself and not to wait for others' "Do" and "Don't":
That is discipline.

When I look up and triumph over every selfish thing,
The things that no one knows about – the cowardly, selfish thing;
And when with heart and will I live to please my glorious King:
That is discipline.

To trample on that curious thing inside me that says 'I';
To think of others always – never, never of that 'I';
To learn to live all to my Saviour's word, 'Deny':
That is discipline.

Amy was to learn discipline at Broughton Grange on an even wider scale. She was immersed in all kinds of work for the Lord in the area, including a Tuesday Evening Scripture Union work, and a Saturday Bible Class for girls. She even got involved in a speaking tour of the Clydeside villages in Scotland with Hannah Govan of the Faith Mission. The very first published article by Amy Carmichael appeared in the Faith Mission magazine, *Bright Words*. It was called *Fightin' Sal* – the story of a Shawlie who had been converted at *The Welcome*. In Belfast today, the Faith Mission bookstore is the most famous Christian bookstore in Ireland, North or South; and carries tens of thousands of Christian books. Its long-time manager, Mr Edward Douglas, is a legend.

In his sermon *The New Name*, George McDonald (who became mentor to C. S. Lewis and G. K. Chesterton) makes a very powerful – even haunting – point about a statement made by Jesus in the Book of Revelation. "He who has an ear, let him hear what the Spirit says to the churches. To him who overcomes I will give some hidden manna to eat. And I will give him a white stone, and on the stone a new name written which no one knows about except him who receives it." What is this name? George McDonald believed that the new name is the communication of what God thinks about a person to that person: in that word, He expresses the character, the nature, and the meaning of the person who bears it. George McDonald believed that, when that person has 'become' his or her name, God will give them the stone with their name on it.

Thinking about McDonald's interpretation, I have been trying to hazard a guess as to what name would be on Amy Carmichael's white stone. *Whistle-blower* would sum up a significant characteristic in her life. *Mother* was a word many were to call her in later life. *Lover* is a word that sums up her relationship with Christ. *Rescuer* would capture the essence of the ministry she was to effect. Yet, for me, the word *Light* best sums up her place in history. Wherever she went, Amy shone as a light set on a hill; and if you came anywhere near her there was no escaping that light. Later in life it was to show up a horrendous practice in India; and, through her writing, it guided millions. It still shines, even into the twenty-first century. Unknown to Amy, God was to take that light and place it far from the beautiful English Lake District where the poetry of Wordsworth, Southey and Coleridge flourished. Amy's poetry was to flourish in

suffering and pain, and she was to build a place of refuge in the midst of it all.

On January 13th 1892, mantling snow had fallen across the Lake District, and as the evening wore on millions of flakes gently covered the forests and hills. On that evening, Amy Carmichael was at *Broughton Grange*, having a look at what she called her *Ask and Receive* book. She had just recently been at the Keswick Convention, where she had asked God for rest from the cry of those who were without Christ overseas. She had asked that she might be given gladness to stay at home, and that others be sent. As the cold snow covered this land, described by Wordsworth as the place where *an intermingling of Heaven's pomp is spread on the ground which British shepherds tread*, a momentous struggle began in the heart of the young, twenty-five year old, Irish woman. She was gripped by two words, spoken by the Saviour of the world, as translated in the Authorized Version of the Bible: *Go ye.* The words were as plain to her as any spoken by a human voice.

Amy referred to her struggle as being like that of one David's mighty men, Benaiah, who had gone down into a pit on a snowy day and slain a lion. She was well aware of what the path of obedience would cost – everything. She had enjoyed good health of late, but the thought, that God might want her overseas, had never once crossed her mind; though the thought of those millions, who had never had a chance to hear the gospel, had been constantly before her. The responsibility for her mother's welfare was very real to her, and the responsibility she now had to Robert Wilson was immediately at hand. Her heart shrank from the pain and ache of what leaving those she loved would mean. But the Lord said *Go*; and on that snowy evening, above the Derwent, Amy Carmichael said "Yes, Lord," to His command. She later famously wrote, "In acceptance lieth peace." It must have been a lonely moment, for such a decision is never easy. She took, what Robert Frost called, 'the road less travelled by', and it did make all the difference.

The next day she sat down to write to her mother, to tell her of her decision; but she felt as if she was stabbing someone she loved. She could not finish the letter until the next day. So, it must have brought immense comfort, when her mother replied with an opening poem:

> He who *hath* led *will* lead
> All through the wilderness.
> He who hath fed will surely feed ...
> He who hath heard thy cry
> Will never close His ear.
> He who hath marked thy faintest sigh
> Will not forget thy tear.
> He loveth always, faileth never,
> So rest on Him today – forever.

Graciously, Amy's mother told her that she was willing to give to the Lord, for His service and glory, what He had lent her for so many years. She told Amy that she had been reading a Bible verse, from Psalm 43:3: *O send out Thy light and Thy truth*; and, as it turned out, that light was going to shine in a very dark place through her daughter's life. Wisely, Robert Wilson accepted Amy's decision, as obedience to his and her Master's call. Others, however, were not so kind. The Wilson boys challenged her action, as a breach of faith to their father. Some Keswick Convention leaders said that Robert

Wilson would be dead before she got through the Mediterranean. Mrs. Carmichael's sisters wondered if Amy had not been enchanted by a foreign land, and wanted to get away to that enchantment. In truth, Amy did not want to go; but she felt she *had* to go in answer to Christ's call. When she responded to that call, it was the Christians who hurt her, not the unconverted.

In 1887 someone had sent a ten-pound note to the Chairman of the Keswick Convention, wanting it to be a nucleus for sending out a 'Keswick Missionary', and a fund was duly set up. In 1892, when Amy eventually offered herself for service with the China Inland Mission, she was the first missionary to be sent and supported by the Keswick Convention. She went to London and was examined by the Mission doctor, who refused to pass her as fit to go to China. So, the 'wild bird child' looked for a way out. For a whole year, Amy found no open window to respond to her call, which remained as clear as ever. Then, in consultation with Robert Wilson, it was decided to write to Rev. Barclay Buxton, who was working for Christ at Matsuye on the West coast of Japan, leading a team of young missionaries. Amy felt she should sail for the Far East as soon as possible, and not wait in England for a reply from Rev. Buxton. In consultation with the China Inland Mission, it was agreed that she should sail on March 3rd 1893 with three C.I.M. missionaries in the Peninsular and Orient's *S.S. Valetta*, and wait in Shanghai for Rev. Buxton's reply. The ship slipped her moorings at Tilbury, and Amy Carmichael sailed away to what would become a life of staggering sacrifice, and the facing down of the powers of Hell.

When Amy was in London, awaiting the decision of the China Inland Mission, Geraldine Guinness, who was to marry Hudson Taylor's son, was also staying at the mission house. She had deeply sympathised with Amy's distress at leaving Robert Wilson, and one day she gave her a folded half-sheet of paper. Inside, Geraldine had highlighted two questions from Scripture. The first was from Mark 10:38, *Can ye drink of the cup that I drink of? and be baptized with the baptism that I am baptized with?* The second was from Psalm 78:19, a question raised by the Children of Israel: *Can God furnish a table in*

the wilderness? To these questions, Geraldine added: "Ye shall, indeed
. . . For *with God* all things are possible." Amy kept that sheet of
paper in her possession for the rest of her life. It is now insect-eaten
and stained, but as Amy's ship headed for the East, the paper was
fresh and its promise absolute.

Carrying Love's Light

5   IT WAS 1893. The year was to bring a unique contribution to the history of the world, which included New Zealand, to its credit, becoming the very first country in which women were allowed to vote in a National Election. In Britain, a new corner was turned politically with the founding of the Independent Labour Party by James Keir Hardie, who supported women's suffrage. At eleven years of age Hardie was a coal miner. He became a passionate supporter of the common people, and was said to burn with indignation at their unmerited suffering. He was a compassionate pacifist.

In 1893 a book was published, entitled *My Arctic Journal*. It was written by Josephine Peary, the wife of the intrepid American Arctic explorer, Robert Peary who, eventually, in 1909 was the first person to reach the North Pole. Josephine had accompanied her husband on several of his expeditions, and she gave birth to their daughter, Marie, in the Arctic. It was in 1893 that the United States Stock Market collapsed: 600 Banks folded, and 15,000 businesses closed their doors. No less than 74 railroads went into Receivership.

However, all was not gloom in the United States in 1893. Some people were literally looking up. Sherbourne Wesley Burnham, the American astronomer, was famous for the discovery of double stars.

In the summer of 1893, he was observing 80 miles north of Chicago, and recommended it as the best site for placing the new Yerkes Observatory. By 1908, Professor Burnham had discovered 1,308 double stars.

They were not twins, but they were significant Irish writers: in 1893 the great poet, W. B. Yeats was editing the works of William Blake, and Oscar Wilde produced his play, *A Woman of No Importance*. Such a description could not be attributed to the subject of this present book. In the hand of God, she was to be a woman of immense importance. Whatever else Amy Carmichael was, her heart and mind were consumed by a passion for passing on the best news the world has ever heard. As she keenly observed all that was happening around her on board the *S.S. Valetta*, her behaviour and thinking were a microcosm of her life. She had always had a profound awareness of place and occasion, and sensed an atmosphere very quickly. All this was being captured in her writing, and her poetry certainly fitted Wordsworth's definition of poetry. He said that it was "emotion recollected in tranquillity." Amy's writing style was often pure poetic prose. She constantly related everything she saw and felt to her Christian faith. Her life showed that, when the Lord Jesus said He was the world's light and that He provides light to live in, He delivers. His light touched every corner of her life.

For example, take this letter sent from the *S.S. Valetta* on March 11th 1893. Amy quotes some lines from a hymn, and then relates them to her surroundings:

"Oh! How great Thy loving kindness,
Vaster, broader than the sea.
Oh! How marvellous Thy goodness,
Lavished all on me.

Upon the Hurricane Deck we sang it one evening as the sun was setting in the great Bay of Biscay. Behind us lay the calm dark waters stretching away and away before us. They shimmered in a glory of colour and gold, above us the glow of eventide, underneath were the everlasting arms of a love limitless as the encompassing ocean. That night we had the beauty of the moonlight. Upon the darkly heaving swell, it rose and fell quietly, peacefully, in silvery loveliness. And as we entered the Mediterranean He commanded His stormy wind to lash the great waters into glorious fury. In the presence of such majesty human speech failed, and through the mighty rush and roar the old Psalm sang, chorus-fashion, over and over, deep down in one's soul. 'The floods have lifted up, O Lord, the floods have lifted up their voice; the floods lift up their waves. The Lord on high is mightier than the noise of mighty waters, yea, than the mighty waves of the sea.'

Last night I stood by the ship's rails looking through the gloaming at the long, long coastline of darkest Africa. Far above, the stars were sparkling, the stars we love at home; in our wake the waters were strung with phosphorus and radiance, but across the dusky distance there glimmered but one small light, whose very presence seemed only to intensify the deep sad darkness beyond. Then, as I stood and watched the shadows deepen round that lovely light, it seemed to shine a mute appeal for its land, which still lay in the darkness of death – the light-bearers so few and far between that today millions and millions whom Jesus died to win are left to live and die alone. O, that His Bride might awaken to the heart-desire of her Bridegroom e'er the cry rings down, 'Go ye forth to meet Him.' Surely, if we go on leaving 'the voiceless silence of despair' unanswered, the heathen whom we might tell untold, we shall have to 'shrink in shame before Him at His coming.'"

As the *S.S. Valetta* headed across the Mediterranean through the Suez Canal and out across the Indian Ocean, Amy did not remain passive to the spiritual needs of the people on board. She got involved in holding a Sunday evening service, and a Bible Reading on deck every morning. The Captain gave permission for evangelistic services in the evenings. Amy had many a spiritual conversation with the passengers and crew; but it was not all plain sailing. In a letter to the Keswick Mission on March 15th 1893, she wrote of an Indian to whom she had been witnessing. She felt he was beginning to see that Jesus must indeed be the Son of God. Here is her report of what he said:

"I have been in your land, I have watched and asked – Oh, yes, many persons, many times – about your Lord Jesus Christ, your Saviour-God. And did I find they loved, cared? No. They turned to grasp money, position, name. Your land is 'Christian', and mine 'Heathen'; but my people worship in earnest. You say false gods? Yes, but they are true in their hearts: what they know, they do. Your people are outside, good and religious, but are they inside here? I looked for them, the true ones who loved and in truth worshipped – did I find them? (With a movement which told of a strong surprise and disappointment), Ah, no!"

Amy challenges her fellow Christians at home to pray for 'Sahib'. There can have been only a very few people on board the *S.S. Valetta* who were unaware of where Amy's heart lay.

Soon another result of the light of Amy Carmichael's tender witness was to emerge. In those days, a voyage to Shanghai involved a change of ship at Colombo in Ceylon. Amy was delighted to meet many of her friends in Colombo, including close friends of the family called the Leichings. In time, they were to be a vital link in her call to India. Amy eventually boarded the *Sutlej*, and found her tiny cabin infested with rats and cockroaches; although she did not believe that a Christian should give thanks for everything, she did paint a text for her cabin which read *In everything give thanks*. Mercifully, the Captain allowed her to sleep on deck under the stars. As the *Sutlej* crossed the China Sea the Captain observed the life and behaviour of Amy Carmichael, and the light of her witness began to penetrate the spiritual darkness in his life. He was drawn to Christ, he said, by seeing the reality that Christ was to Amy. Before his ship reached its destination, the Captain had become a Christian.

On arrival in the great port of Shanghai, it must have been a huge relief for Amy to find letters awaiting her at the China Inland Mission Home, offering her a warm welcome when she would arrive in Japan. What if there had been none? But Amy didn't inhabit the country called Doubt; faith was her landscape.

When the tug from the steamer in which Amy had crossed the Sea of Japan landed her at the Port of Shimonoseki, there was a storm raging. The missionary sent to meet her had been delayed by the storm and, much to her amusement (believe it or not!), when Amy found no one to greet her she literally sat down and laughed. I wonder what I would have done? For an hour 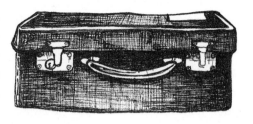 the Wild-bird child from Millisle sat in a dark room with her baggage piled high around her, trying to explain her problem to a crowd who did not understand a word she was saying. Rescued by a passing American, she eventually found her friends.

Fifty-six years later, Amy recalled in her writing a walk she had with a missionary on the beach at Shimonoseki. The missionary discovered that Amy thought that all missionaries loved one another, which she found incredulous. But Amy did believe that they loved one another; so when she discovered that they did not always do so, she thought of the instruction of the Saviour when He asked His followers to love one another fervently with a pure heart. That walk on a Japanese beach revealed to her that not everyone 'walked the talk'.

Amy settled into her Christian service at Matsuye, and set about learning what is arguably the most difficult language in the world. Again, her lovely gift of observation and spiritual application was poured into her writing. In a letter dated January 2nd 1893, even Japanese glow-worms and fireflies came in for the Carmichael touch.

"We have lovely glow-worms and fireflies in Japan. In the still dark night they shine in the ferny hedges and flit away like living lamps to the darker depths behind. So clear is their fiery light that by one I can see to read. They say so much to me – these silent shining things – oh, to be His glow-worm, hidden where only He sees in some quiet hedge of His planting, lighting it up for Him; or, if He will, His firefly – carrying His love-light over the hedge if He beckons so far away, where He goeth before. Oh that the stillness in which only His lights can shine may ever surround us – oh that in this dark world we may shine – "so shine" that others may see to read His love in the face of our lovely Lord Jesus."

As a biographer, sitting for hours on end reading Amy Carmichael's original letters in the *Public Record Office of Northern Ireland*, I have found that some of their contents are now indelibly etched on my mind. I was captivated by a letter from Matsuye, dated June 11th 1893. It perfectly encapsulates a day in the life of this great Christian. It has drawings that Amy made of what she observed, and her letter bursts with creativity and spirituality.

She describes going with a colleague for a day's 'seed sowing' among the villages at the head of the lake. Together they take the steamboat across the lake, and she describes the breeze, the blue water, the fleecy clouds; and how it all merges into 'a sort of shimmering loveliness'. Their basket of books becomes 'a basket of seeds'. As the pair begin to distribute their literature, Amy tells of one who 'read aloud slowly and wonderingly the strange new story they had never heard before.' She writes, 'Some did not even know the name Christianity – much less its meaning.' They walked the ten miles back to Matsuye, 'sowing and praying as we went along.' Her colleague's feet became so sore that she walked in her stocking soles; but Amy, afraid of much darning, kept her shoes on. It is a very human letter.

They met a Japanese wedding crowd and a funeral, and both receive Amy's analysis! By the end of the letter, as the lights of Matsuye come into view, I have found that that day has become part of my unforgettable memories. Her feelings become the feelings of her reader. In Amy Carmichael's life, every day was so full of purpose. Nothing was seen as happening by chance: everything was linked with her calling to serve Jesus Christ.

One interesting characteristic of Amy's witness was the fact that she decidedly turned against using pictures of the Lord Jesus as an aid to her communication of the gospel. One day she heard a little girl talking about 'magic lantern' slides, which were to be shown later that evening. "They will show us their God," she said. While Amy had been impressed with the lovely picture of Christ that she knew as a child, she came to believe that in a land filled with millions of gods such as Japan, and later India, such pictures were inappropriate. She never tried to influence anyone in the matter, but fervently believed that the Holy Spirit could reveal the exquisite beauties of Christ to human hearts and minds way beyond any human attempt. Implicitly she trusted in the Holy Spirit to reveal Christ through human witness. It was a private conviction, shared only by a few; and one cannot but admire her for it, and her wisdom to hold it quietly, while working with others who may not all have been of the same opinion.

Bishop Frank Houghton reckons that there is a hint that someone may have fallen in love with Amy at this time in her life. Bishop Houghton records that, over 40 years later, she wrote about an experience she had during a Missionary Conference in Japan. He quotes Amy's description of this experience:

"On this day many years ago I went away alone to a cave in a mountain called Arima. I had feelings of fear about the future. That was why I went there – to be alone with God. The devil kept on whispering, 'It's alright now, but what about afterwards? You are going to be very lonely.' And he painted pictures of loneliness – I can see them still and I turned to my God in a kind of desperation, and said, 'Lord, what can I do? How can I go on to the end?' And He said, 'None of them that trust in Me shall be desolate.' That word has been with me ever since. It has been fulfilled to me. It will be fulfilled to you."

Elizabeth Elliot, in her deeply thoughtful and inspiring biography of Amy Carmichael entitled *A Chance to Die*, also records what Amy had confided in her Indian Secretary, Neela: "A letter had come on the eve of her sailing for Japan. She did not say who wrote it. She did not say it was a proposal. She said merely that it "looked towards what you call 'the other life.'" She waited quietly. "Deep down in me a voice seemed to be saying, 'No, no, no. I have something different for you to do.'" She held to that word when her woman's heart longed for a man's love. That day in the cave in Arima, Japan, was one of those days – a day full of fear of a lonely future, when the Voice spoke again: 'None of them that trust in Me shall be desolate.'"[1]

One pictures Amy alone in that cave, on the other side of the earth from her native Ireland. Far now from the beach at Millisle; and the hundreds of people on the Shankill Road in Belfast, who loved her for who she was and what she did. She struggled with the cost of following what she believed was God's will for her life: who knows just how agonising those moments were? The fear of a lonely end to her life stabbed her heart, but she clutched the promise of God. I think she deliberately gave up the opportunity of marriage and children for Christ and His gospel; but she could not have known that, by the end of her life of incredible usefulness, she would have hundreds of children. In what sense? In the sense that Christ spoke of when He said, *Assuredly, I say to you, there is no one who has left house, or brothers, or sisters, or father, or mother, or wife, or children, or lands, for My sake, and the gospel's, who shall not receive a hundredfold now in this time, houses, and brothers, and sisters, and mothers, and children, and lands, with persecutions; and in the age to come eternal life* (Mark 10:29-30).

The little girl who had sung a hymn as her boat had headed for the dangerous bar at the mouth of Strangford Lough, the young woman who had lived in the beautiful *Broughton Grange* and gazed on the matchless fells of the Lake District all around her, was being called now in a Japanese cave to follow the Lord Jesus wherever He might lead. She later wrote:

Deep to deep answereth now;
Dimly I see a cross –
Thirst, wounds, thorn-crowned brow,
Stripping, and utmost loss.
Over the bar the fret of the foam,
Rain on the fell where the young lambs roam;
Lord, art Thou bidding me
Call thy little ones, call thy little ones Home?

Echoes from that cave at Arima, Japan, in the nineteenth century, have reached me in the twenty-first century. Just recently, I had a phone call from another missionary who had worked with Amy

Carmichael. Her name is Margaret Wilkinson, and she now lives in retirement in Castlerock, a little seaside town in Co. Londonderry. She told me how she had known Amy Carmichael at the later stage of the great missionary's life, but she didn't refer to her as 'Amy'. I could not help noticing that she freely, naturally, and affectionately called her 'Mother'. Selah.

When The 'D' In Disappointment Becomes An 'H'

6

IT WAS 1894. On December 3rd, the remarkable writer Robert Louis Stevenson was reading the latest chapter from his novel *Weir of Hermiston* to his wife, Fanny. He then went back to work on the novel, dictated some letters in the afternoon, and went for a swim. After a change of clothes, he came down the staircase of *Vailima*, his Samoan home, and suggested his wife make a 'Vailima Salad'. He then stood on the verandah, talking happily to Fanny, helping her to mix the oil and lime juice. Suddenly he fell to his knees in pain, and soon lost consciousness. He died at 8.10 p.m. that evening.

That very same month found another writer, one Amy Wilson-Carmichael, at *Broughton Grange* in Cumbria. It was a year that had seen Japan go to war with China over Korea. Nicholas II became Tsar of Russia, and Edward VIII was born. Norman Rockwell, the distinguished American artist, first saw the light of day; the second, and formidable, President of the United States, John Quincy Adams, died. After a nightmare journey, Amy arrived at *Broughton Grange* for Christmas 1894. What on earth had happened during the previous almost-fifteen months in Japan?

There are many remarkable stories that could be told about it, and of her life with her interpreter, travelling companion and teacher, a Japanese Christian called Misaki San. There is the story of how Amy and Misaki San visited the home of a man whom people believed was possessed with six fox spirits. He was strapped and bound to two heavy beams laid crosswise on the floor. When Amy and her friend visited the home, and Amy spoke of the power of the Lord Jesus to cast out the spirits, the man went into a paroxysm of rage. He raved and cursed, and tried to get at Amy and Misaki San, so they were hurried out of the room. Amy told the man's wife that they would go home and pray, and asked her to let them know if he was delivered of the fox spirits. An hour later a messenger arrived to say the foxes had gone, the cords were off, and the man was asleep. The next day the man sent for Amy and her friend. The transformation was awesome. He gave Amy a branch of pomegranate in flower, and for Amy pomegranates were never to be the same again! He was later converted to Jesus Christ.

There were many answers to prayer and good work done for the Lord Jesus in those months in Japan; but Amy began to suffer acute neuralgia. She wrote to her mother explaining that the climate was affecting her brain, and her eyes in particular. She was ordered by the doctor to take a long rest. He diagnosed her as suffering from what was known as 'Japanese head', a painful malady to which foreigners were often susceptible. Amy went to Shanghai, where she was given a room by the China Inland Mission. Writing from Shanghai on July 11th 1894, Amy shows her deep respect for the Japanese people. She writes of their "airy, lightsome, cleanly little dwellings," and this "laughter loving people . . . the Japanese are strong in mental power at all events, and if they will only retain, and prize as it deserves, their own beautiful national life, they will surely be all the more truly great."

She makes a captivating comment in what she now calls her *Scrapperie*, a letter home to her supporters. The *Scraps* of Belfast's College Gardens was now coming into its own! Her comment concerns the huge immensity of China and its spiritual need, which crushed and bewildered her.

"The mind fails to grasp what the eye reads so easily. We know all the calculations planned to make it real to us. We know them, but we don't take them in. One which appeals to me most, perhaps because it is so simple and yet so awfully profound, is the fact that, while it would take 17 years for all of China's millions to pass in single file, passing 30 miles a day – 17 years, think of it – all those gathered in by Protestant missions could pass you in one day. For 17 years the dark procession must pass you in darkness – stay! They do pass you, whether you will or no. Stand still and think. Do you not see them passing? Do you not hear the tread of those feet?"

Amy then pleads with her readers to do whatever they can to swell the numbers of those converted to Christ, and adds these rather haunting words:

"But as I write the words I remember with a dull weight of pain, which seems to paralyse heart and pen – unless God works a miracle, most who read these lines will hear no trump of feet, hear no call for help; for them the sun will shine as if it shone on Summer anywhere. They will read on, and care no more:

By other signs the world is one
Than that which wails from Macedon,
The roar of gain is round it rolled,
Or men unto themselves are sold
And cannot list the alien cry,
'Oh hear us, help us, lest we die!'"

On July 18th, it was laid on Amy's heart that, as the next step, God had prepared a work for her in Ceylon. God, who had spoken to her so clearly in her room at *Broughton Grange*, was speaking clearly again. Confirmations of His direction began to follow. She fully realised that not everyone would see the situation as she did, and she wrote pages of explanation home. She had no house in Japan and no settled work; and was now convinced that God was telling her to move on. She sailed for Colombo on July 28th 1894, having written ahead to the eldest of a group of young women who had been working with her friends, Mr. and Mrs. Leiching. Sadly, both husband and wife had died of fever within days of each other. Amy's coming to those courageous young women was seen as an answer to their prayers. Her voyage cost her £10, and she was escorted by a kindly Church Missionary Society missionary who was travelling to Palestine.

Amy was tenderly welcomed by her friends at the Heneratgoda Village Mission, and immediately began to work with them for Christ. The new missionary was welcomed by more than the other missionaries. In *Scrapperie* No. 16, August 25th 1894, she writes of being 'gloriously interrupted' on three separate intervals:

"Three tiny brown hands pressed bunches of flowers inside, and three pairs of tiny brown eyes smiled up at mine. They are the most captivating little pets, these dear little Brownies – a great contrast to the quaint little dotes of Japan and the queer little imps of China, these wee things have eyes which glow and shine, hair which tosses about in curls or falls strangled, and silky round shapely little heads, pretty shy ways and graceful limbs – brown, all brown. The flowers they bring are too exquisite for telling – Ixopia, today's are, scarlet, embedded in soft green, and a delicate creamy thing, sweet and scented, new to me, and pure white Gardenia, that treasure of home green houses."

And on another occasion,

"This morning a mite of a boy brought me a big bunch of plantains (bananas). As I took him on my knee, he said softly, 'I give you,' which much I could fortunately understand."

She lived in a cottage in a malarial jungle village, and one evening, following the conversion of a Buddhist woman, a very angry man arrived at the cottage brandishing a knife. The two eldest women and Amy knelt on the floor and prayed. The man swept the knife over their heads and then went away. Amy writes of all kinds of hassles, including workmen who proved frustratingly untrue to their word: now they were coming, now they weren't. Amidst the frustration of the workmen, who had promised to put in floors, "a floor upon which things jump . . . and not to say the muddiness of my surroundings right now" – in a *Scrapperie* of September 14th 1894, she suggests, "as a creature takes colour from its environment, my *Scrapperie* will probably be extremely subliminary."

Subliminary?! I reckon her letter contains one of the most moving descriptions of Christian witness that I have ever been privileged to read. With all my heart, I ask my readers to think long on what it intends to convey. "Change the D in disappointment into an H," writes God's fresh messenger to Heneratgoda , Ceylon. "I must not forget to tell you such a lovely little ANSWER we got the other day:

It was very much upon my heart that we ought to reach the Buddhist priests. The girls said they had never gone to their place. It was not allowed, and women never went; but "every creature" included Buddhist priests. Here, where there were no men, we were responsible to obey in so far as in us lay. So we went. As we walked along the beautiful palm-shaded road, we prayed that He, whose sent ones we were, should clearly go before us and guard us from certain dangers the girls felt might meet us. Here it is not as in Japan, where one is safe anywhere. I find it hard to realise this, but so it is. We never go any distance alone, we never stay out after dark. One day I was greatly longing for a quiet time away from everybody, and thought of going some little distance to secure it, as often I used to at Matsuye; but Jessie would not let me, and I had to believe she was right. At last we got to the precincts of the Temple near where the priests' house stood. As we climbed over the stile and found ourselves within that 'sacred' confine, we knew we were taking a step for which His Word was our only warrant. But it was enough.

A barking dog was the first lion in the way. A voice called him off. We went on unmolested to the front of the verandah, and saw the priest sitting there, and heard him say to the dog 'be quiet'. So we knew it was he who had called him away, instead of setting him on us. 'Praise the Lord,' whispered Jessie.

The verandah was a long, low one. Upon a chair covered with a white cloth (a sign of honour), sat the priest in his yellow robe, fan in hand, chewing Betel. He did not look at all holy, nor was his occupation particularly refined. Everybody chews Betel here; but I did not expect to find a priest so engaged. (Betel is the nut of the tropical palm tree, *areca*, and forms the basis of the stimulant, Betel chew, which has a reputation as a panacea and tonic throughout Asia. In India, it has been integrated within the social and religious system.)[1] Beside him stood an acolyte, also in a yellow robe but minus a fan. He was reading in a slow chant from some sacred book, and all about stood silent listeners. They looked at us, the boy stopped reading, and the priest said in English 'Good morning'. It was evening then, but English words were welcome. I asked him (in English) if we might stay for a few minutes and speak to him, as we had come with a message for him, and he said 'Oh yes, stay'. We sat down on the low steps, our position being inferior to his, and, thinking he would understand best in his own language, Anna, who speaks it well, began to talk to him. But he argued and talked her down. The people around were delighted. We tried through interpretation, he scoffed at it all, and would not hear us through a sentence; then I tried, as a last resource, English alone. How the girls prayed – it was our last chance.

He was perfectly silent – the listener. I felt as though their prayers were closing his lips, holding his tongue still. Every moment he looked as if he were on the point of beginning again, but he didn't. In the simplest words I knew, I put the truth before him and witnessed unto Christ our Saviour, Keeper, King. He never spoke till I ceased, and then, without waiting for more talking, we came straight away. It was as solemn a five minutes as ever I spent. Oh how one had to trust for every word – how thankful one was for the practice in simple speaking (speaking without unnecessary words, which complicate the sense so, to one who knows so little English) the year in Japan had given. Without it, one would not so readily have bought up every possibility of that priceless opportunity.

Will you pray for that soul? Will one of you take him as your Prayer-Tryst? God does not lead us like that for nothing. He means something for him. Someone who can, please pray for him."

The particular charm of Amy Carmichael (though she would have abhorred the word) entrances her readers in the next few paragraphs of her letter. Here is Amy, wholly committed to spreading the Good News of the Lord Jesus at every opportunity.

Here she is, incarnating herself into another culture, far removed from her Ulster upbringing, summoning up undeniable courage in the face of formidable obstacles. She epitomises the truth, pointed out by C. S. Lewis, that those who think most about the next world are those who most influence this one. Yet, at the same time, Amy is able to meticulously observe and rapturously enjoy the natural world around her. She continues her story:

"Coming home we saw a chameleon. I wasn't sure of the spelling of that word, and looked it up. To my amusement the little 'dictioney' states that it is 'an animal said to take the colour of whatever it is applied to, and (erroneously) to live on air'. Evidently a slightly fabulous beasty; one can imagine it floating hugely in the good man's mind, as he penned the doubtful description thereof. A sort of twin cousin of the 'Phenex' (as he spells it), I see he describes it in much the same fashion (he most probably considered it to be relegated to the realm of myth).

But it is real for all that – a long lizard-like creature with a tail ending in a thread and a sort of comb in its head which it can erect at pleasure. When we first saw it, it was bright emerald green with darker shadings down the back, and its head was iris crimson, exactly the colouring around it, for the bush on which it sat had some 'Autumn leaves' in glow, among the green. As we watched it, it faded softly, and as we nearer drew it vanished – which sounds ghostly enough for one little dictioney's compiler, but is not so intended. I mean to get one for a pet – or a study, and then you may expect morals by the yard."

In October 1894, Rev. Barclay Buxton, the leader of the Christian work in which Amy had been involved in Japan, had been on furlough when Amy left Japan. He compassionately and courteously wrote to her, saying that he accepted God's leading in her life, and thanked her for all she had meant to the work. It is significant that he pointed out how she had been an influence of love and unity. He was truly a big-hearted man, was the Rev. Buxton. He asked Amy, now that she was distanced from the work in Japan, that if she had a word from the Lord about it, to tell it to him plainly. His action took the application of much grace. Barclay Buxton's big-heartedness is now a very memorable nectar from his faithful life of Christian service.

Amy applied herself to learning the Singhalese language. All seemed settled for a work in Ceylon, the land of the chameleons, when, on November 27th 1894, she received a letter from home, telling her that Robert Wilson had suffered a stroke and was very ill. Amy did not hesitate. The man who had become her surrogate father needed her. Borrowing some warm clothing, within an hour she set out for Colombo and secured a passage to London. She sailed the next day.

We must never think that Amy Carmichael lived life on impulses. In no way! She saw her reaction to this undeniable crisis

as the fulfilling of a duty. In fact, as she took the mammoth journey to England she was ill, fearful, and alone. A station official had to actually get her out of a train in Rome, and put her on the train to Paris. She called him 'that Roman Angel'! Because she was so ill, there were bits of the journey that she could not remember. Coming out of one of those bouts, she was comforted by an old Frenchman who took pity on her and promised to pilot her across Paris, where they changed trains for Calais. He was called 'the French Angel'!

Amy's mother met her in London the day before her 27th birthday. Still ill, she was taken to the home of friends and given medical attention. Within ten days, she took the journey to the Lake District. Once again, she was in the land where Wordsworth had climbed the fells in Summer, skated on the lakes in Winter, and immortalised it all in verse. At last, she arrived safely at *Broughton Grange*, as many of the farmers and shepherds, the townsfolk and people of the Lake District, were celebrating the birth of Christ. The surrounding mountains enfolded Amy, as the door closed behind her in what was to her one of the dearest homes on earth.

7 Of Churchill, And The Mad Riders Of Kotagiri

THE YEAR WAS 1895. As with all other years in history, it had its share of birth and death. It saw the death of the man who set the stage for biology and biochemistry. Louis Pasteur solved the mysteries of rabies, anthrax, chicken cholera and silk worm diseases, and contributed to the development of the first vaccines. Guglielmo Marconi, a self-taught 21 year old from Bologna, gave birth to the radio, to the sound of a rifle shot. Scientists and other experts held that electromagnetic waves could only be transmitted in a straight line; and then only if there was nothing in the way. They thought the main obstacle was the curvature of the earth's surface, but Marconi proved them wrong by placing a transmitter near his house and a receiver behind a hill 2km away. He put his brother Alfonso, his chief assistant, in charge of a 'receiving party' of estate workers, who stood by the receiver. It was decided that the transmission was to be confirmed by a rifle shot. On a golden September day, Marconi heard Alfonso's single gunshot echoing down the valley, confirming that, for the first time in history, the three dots of the letter 'S' of the Morse Alphabet had travelled through space.

Marconi found that there was little enthusiasm in Italy for his invention. The appropriate Government Minister considered it not to be suitable for telecommunications. Marconi later astonished the world by sending wireless signals over the Atlantic from Poldhu, Cornwall, to St. John's, Newfoundland. His invention soon extended to the four corners of the earth, and in 1909 he was awarded the Nobel Prize for Physics.

In the India of 1895, the British Raj (or, rule) had just about reached its flood tide. Its echoes are preserved in the English language by such words as bazaar, bungalow, verandah, sandals, gingham, jodhpurs, pyjamas, punch, khaki, and chit. The Indian Mutiny of 1856 had seen the power of the Honourable East India Company transferred to the British Crown. The Empire of the Raj consisted of 602 States, and was ruled from London, which was at that time the capital of the world, and the largest metropolis history had ever known. These States were ruled under the principle of 'paramountcy' – a mixture of paternalism and dictatorship, where the rights of the rajas, who governed India, were respected by the Queen's Viceroy. The Union Jack flew over all public buildings, and the pukka sahib and the burrah sahib were masters.

In all, the British spent 350 years in India; but their eventual colonial rule was but a temporary interruption in the astounding continuity of Indian history. There was an India before the Europeans came; and there most certainly is one now. It is worth remembering that *Sanskrit*, the oldest living language on earth, entered India in the 2nd millennium BC.

On the burning plains of Sind, in what is now Pakistan, an empire once traded with cities like Ur and Babylon. At the time of Egypt's pyramid age, this empire had the biggest city in the world, and the most widespread civilisation. India's most brilliant scientific invention was the mathematical system, which we all use today. A young Indian prince whom we call Buddha was alive and teaching at the same time as Pythagoras and Isaiah the Prophet.

A Mauryan Emperor called Asoka began ruling in India at 13 years of age. He ruled from 268-232 BC; and during the early part of his reign he carried on a fierce and bloodthirsty campaign to bring the whole of India under his control. On his conversion to Buddhism he deeply repented of his past violence, and introduced in India his doctrine of non-violence that is part of many people's belief to this day.

In the 16th Century the Moguls came, introducing the famous art which we identity with India. Akbar 'The Great', a Mogul emperor, came to recognise three things that were vital for a stable empire: a fair rent, a land ruled by men who were impartial and responsible to himself, and the importance of Muslim and Hindu living at peace with one another. The village life of Akbar's day still survives today: two thirds of India's population – some 850 millions – live in village communities.

The Tamils of South India traded spices for gold with the Greeks and Romans, and searched deeply for unity amid diversity. 'Pepper' and 'ginger' are South Indian words.

The clash between Western and Indian civilisation was deep. Individualism and rationality are important in Western civilisation. India is big on renunciation and the inner life. Even in the twenty-first century, poetry is the biggest attraction for mass audiences.

For a century and a half, the British administered the sub-continent of India, and finally they spent thirty years deliberately transferring power. Sadly, the British, who came from a small island five thousand miles away, often treated the Indians – the descendants of one of the oldest civilisations on earth – like children. They plundered their animals and trees, and were often truly arrogant. Yet, not all English men and women abused their privileges; some came to deeply love India, and treated the Indian people with respect and fairness. It is widely recognised that the Indian Civil Service under the Raj was broadly incorrupt and above bribery. The Raj irrigated the land, founded Indian Universities, built railways, established newspapers, and introduced the concept of Western justice. Hospitals, doctors, and Public Health Officials treated all patients alike, whatever the colour of their skin.

In truth, though, "The British were in India, never of India," wrote Louis Fischer, "masters in somebody else's home." Fischer accurately states: "Imperialism is government of other people, by other people, and for other people. What the subjects gain, be it ever so great, is only the by-product of efforts on behalf of a distant master." Imperialism begets local nationalism; and the years of British imperialism in India were to be demolished by the most improbable, non-violent nationalist in history. In his biography of Gandhi, Fischer states, "He was a private citizen, without wealth, official post, academic distinction, scientific achievement or artistic gift." Gandhi died by an assassin's bullet on January 30th 1948. On his death, the Indian Government received 3,411 messages of sympathy from foreign countries. "Mahatma Gandhi was the spokesman for the conscience of all mankind," said the United States Secretary of State, George C. Marshall. [4] The United Nations lowered its flag and, Fischer comments, "so did humanity." [5] "Gandhi made humility and simple truth more powerful than empires," wrote the United States Senator, Arthur H. Vandenburg. [6] The last British Viceroy of India, Lord Mountbatten, hoped that Gandhi's life might "inspire our troubled world to save itself by following his noble example." [7] "I know of no other man of any time, or indeed in recent history," wrote Sir Stafford Cripps, "who so forcefully and convincingly demonstrated the power of spirit over material things." [8] The last statement could be argued over, for sure; and I would like to continue to vouch for a European woman who most certainly demonstrated such a characteristic!

Robert Wilson had recovered, and Amy, of course, never had any intention of staying in England. On July 26th 1895, at an informal Committee meeting in Keswick, Amy Carmichael was accepted for service in India with the Church of England Zenana Missionary Society. The following day she spoke at a Missionary Meeting in the big tent of the Keswick Convention, unrolling a blue riband with the words emblazoned upon it, "Nothing too precious for Jesus." If ever anybody 'walked the talk,' Amy was that person. She poured out her life for the Lord Jesus, never returning from India. Fifty-six years later she died there, not only in it but of it.

The month of December 1895 found Amy Carmichael in Bangalore, India, as a Christian missionary with the Church of England Zenana Missionary Society. It was founded in 1852 by Lady

Mary Jane Kinnard, its aim being for women to reach women for Christ in India. In Asia as a whole, cultural restrictions meant that no men (not even physicians) could reach out to women in need. The word *Zenana* is a Hindi word for that part of a house where women were kept in seclusion. There were both men and women on the Mission Board, but only women missionaries served with the Mission. Later the Mission became known as *The Bible and Medical Missionary Fellowship*, and now *Interserve* (*InterServe* in the United States) *International*. It has National Councils, Committees or auxiliaries in seventeen countries, with its International Office on the island of Cyprus. It truly is an international and interdenominational fellowship of Christians, committed to each other in partnership, for service to the peoples of South and Central Asia and the Middle East.

In a letter to her family from the Zenana Hospital, Bangalore, dated January 3rd 1896, Amy describes the hospital in which she had a room as "a big army barracks-like place, built high and dry in a sandy compound on a slope above the town. It will look nicer soon I hope, when the trees grow up round it, and creepers (but to this the Medical Powers demur!) festoon its bare granite walls. I am to be its 'Prophet' (and I have a veritable Prophet's Chamber). There will be endless work to do." By 'Prophet', Amy meant that she was the hospital Evangelist, and she described her work as "most interesting, and I am most grateful for deliverance from bungalow life!"

In the Bangalore of 1896, while Amy gave herself to her work at the hospital and settled down to serious language study, beginning with Urdu, and later, Tamil, another had arrived from England, and was likewise giving himself to study. That winter, Lieutenant Winston Spencer Churchill, a subaltern in the 4th Hussars of the British Army, was approaching twenty-two years of age. His first grasp of Indian soil had dislocated his shoulder. The shore-boat that brought him into Bombay had dropped away as he had eagerly gripped a large iron ring. This gave him a life-long disability for tennis, and a chronic tendency to go out of action at odd moments – including his unduly expansive gestures at the House of Commons.

It was in 1896 that the 4th Hussars moved South from Bombay, to permanent quarters outside Bangalore. In the six long hours during which the sun beat down upon Southern India – between morning parade and evening polo, at which he was the star – Winston resolved to "read history, philosophy, economics and things like that; and I wrote to my mother asking for such books as I heard of on these topics." [9] Why this sudden transformation in the young Winston?

Why this thirst for reading and study, when he could have enjoyed the comradeship of the privileged class to which he belonged?

On the day Winston's troop-ship left Southampton, a friend told him, "Christ's Gospel is the last word in Ethics." [10] Churchill wondered what on earth Ethics was. He assumed that it meant the Public School spirit: honourable behaviour, playing the game, or even patriotism. Then, somebody else on board the troop-ship told him that Ethics dealt not merely with <u>what</u> you ought to do, but with <u>why</u> it ought to be done; and that there was a huge amount of literature on the subject. "Here, in Bangalore, there is no one to tell me about Ethics, for love or money," Winston commented. [11] Obviously, he hadn't crossed the path of the Evangelist from Ireland over at the Zenana Mission Hospital!

Winston Churchill also realised that his knowledge of history was limited. He set himself to respond to the intellectual hunger and curiosity that was growing within him. He began with Gibbon's eight-volume *Decline and Fall of the Roman Empire*. This was followed by Reade's *The Martyrdom of Man* and Plato's *Republic*; then twelve volumes of Macaulay's *History*. He covered fifty pages of Macaulay and twenty-five pages of Gibbon every day. Now he was reading three or four books a time, "to avoid tedium"; pouring over Schopenhauer, Darwin, Aristotle, Malthus, William Lecky's *European*

Morals, Pascal's *Provincial Letters*, Adam Smith's *Wealth of Nations*, and Hallam's *Constitutional History*. He asked his mother to send him all one hundred volumes of the *Annual Register* – Burke's record of public events. He explained to her that he wanted to know the detailed Parliamentary history of the last one hundred years. So, his mother, Jenny, sent him twenty-seven volumes at fourteen shillings each. He explained that the *Annual Register* would arm him with a "sharp sword," and Macaulay, Gibbon, Plato, etc. would "train the muscles to wield that sword to greatest effect." [12]

Churchill later wrote that all this reading caused him to pass through "a violent and aggressive anti-religious phase, which, had it lasted, might have made me a nuisance." [13] It is interesting to note that he resolved the problem by his experience of the power of prayer. His nurse, Elizabeth Ann Everest, who had begun taking care of him when he was one month old, was a Kentish lady with strong 'Low Church' views. She was his comforter and strength, and a source of deep understanding and security. Mrs. Everest taught the young Winston to recite prayers at her knee; and he recited them in moments of danger in his life. So, he began to learn the power of prayer, and determined never to discard the reasoning of the heart for that of the head. He enjoyed both, and discovered that God answered his prayers.

I am no film director, but if I were, I would love to film the juxtaposition of Amy Wilson Carmichael and Winston Spencer Churchill in Bangalore, 1896. God was moulding a man to become Freedom's champion in one of the darkest hours in World History; and he was moulding a woman, awesomely to stand against one of the cruellest of all human sins. Neither knew their ultimate destiny, any more than the rest of us do; but their common bond was that they both believed in the power of prayer. One of them would be used to help bring down the heinous monster, Hitler; and the other, the disgusting cruelty of child abuse.

One wonders if Churchill ever rode out by the racecourse during his year in Bangalore. If so, he could hardly have missed seeing a rather regular equestrian event! Queen Victoria's representative in the state of Mysore was called The Resident (though, in 1881, the actual administration of the City had been given to the Maharaja of Mysore). Amy, who often rode her pony in the area, used to race the Residency carriage round the racecourse and up the long hill that led to the cantonments near where she lived! Later she wrote about how she did dozens of similar "mad things" at that time. She writes of being "not in the least good and sober-minded." In truth, she was extremely lonely at this time, and often frustrated by the wider missionary establishment around her. Under duress, she went to the Nilgiris Hills, where many of the British and missionaries went in the oppressive heat of April and May. They were expected to travel by Sedan Chairs, which involved sitting on a *dholi*, a small stool suspended from poles, carried on the shoulders of coolies. Amy and the hospital doctor decided they would ride on ponies to the Nilgiris. They went first to Kotagiri, and there Amy let her hair down – literally. In the evenings she went out riding, hatless, with her hair flowing freely. She and her fellow-riders became known as 'the mad riders of Kotagiri'.

She described graphically what happened on two of these occasions:

"We came upon the elite of the little place, residents and visitors, congregated on the road. There was the good old Bishop and his sister, and the Bishop-to-be, his wife and various ladies and Middles, and perambulators enclosing babies, and a dog or two. The small crowd parted with alacrity as we shot through, and we caught a fleeting glance of the gaze of astonishment and horror. There are two very mild old gentlemen who are fond of taking their walks abroad, round the hill that we consider our cantering-row. We delight to amble sedately past them, then, a yard or two ahead, break into our wildest gallop and they remain behind in a state of apoplexy …"

"Once I ran over a man. I did not mean to – he wouldn't get out of the way and one can't stop short in mid-gallop. Lillian reported him not hurt, only somewhat surprised. And this will be over soon. When one is ready for work, a bullock cart will be the order of the day. Just now I take it as an extra good gift which helps to keep me strong for the months of grind before me."

The little girl – once thrown by her horse, and lying stunned beside the sea wall in Millisle, who had later taken her pony and trap vigorously around the lanes and roads of Cockermouth and district, raced the Residency Carriage around the racecourse at Bangalore, and whose riding was shattering the peace and quiet of the British establishment at Kotagiri in the Nilgiris Hills – was never, ever going to become an establishment figure! She was a Christian soldier at heart and did not shrink from battle. Soon all her passion and energy, her defiance of easy living and toothless Christianity, would combine by the Spirit's power and leading to make a full-scale assault on the very gates of Hell. Those gates, of course, are defensive, and not offensive: they can be driven back. The issues of the British in India so powerfully dealt with by E. M. Forster in his novel *A passage to India* pale in significance with the reality of the story of Amy Carmichael as it was to unfold.

Bangalore's population is now approaching eight million. It is one of the fastest-growing cities in Asia, and a major scientific research centre at the cutting edge of India's huge technological revolution. But in the 1880's Bangalore was known as *The Garden City*. With its gentle climate, broad streets, and green public parks, it was very popular with Senior Citizens, VIP's and Film Stars, who continued until well after Independence to buy or build dream houses in its urban idyll, and attend its cinemas and theatres.

Amy Carmichael was soon to leave Bangalore's Zenana Hospital and her evangelistic work there. Interestingly, it would all come about through someone whom she had decided she did not like.

Beethoven And The Scale-Strummer

8

IT WAS 1897. Crete declared union with Greece, and the King of Korea proclaimed himself Emperor. Anthony Eden was born, and Johannes Brahms died. Sir Henry Tate donated the Tate Gallery to the people of London, Matisse painted *Dinner Table*, and H. G. Wells published *The Invisible Man*. The Sultan of Zanzibar abolished slavery, J. J. Thomson discovered the electron, and the Victorian era was reaching its zenith in England with the Queen's Diamond Jubilee.

In those days, sea power was everything. At its height there were three hundred and thirty imperial war ships in Britain's Navy, manned by the Navy's ninety-two thousand 'tars', guaranteeing that trade was kept free and the world's waterways were policed. Families who could afford it clothed their children in sailor suits and sailor dresses, with their caps bearing the name of the Queen's latest battleship. Between the 1850's and 1890's, steam power would cut the journey time from England to Capetown, from forty-two days to nineteen days. At no other time in history has any power ever rivalled Britain's sea power in the mid-nineteenth century. If there was a problem anywhere in the Empire, Britain sent a gunboat.

In 1887, Queen Victoria had been very pleased when Parliament bestowed on her the title *Empress of India*. It was at her own suggestion, but she never went there. Instead, a touch of India came to her. In the 1880's her favourite servant was an Indian named Abdul Karim, also known as Munchi, or Teacher. He came with her in 1887 to Osborne on the Isle of Wight, one of her favourite residences. Downstairs in the Household Wing was Queen Victoria's telegraph office. Here she regularly read messages from India that were now able to reach her in a matter of hours. Since the bloody Indian Mutiny of 1857, which had brought about a deep clash of civilisations, and had been, in Indian opinion, 'a war in the cause of religion', Victoria read her telegrams from India very carefully indeed.

The Queen-Empress added a new wing to Osborne House, the centrepiece of which was the spectacular Durbar Room. Inspired by the ornately carved interiors of Mogul palaces, the work was overseen by Lockwood Kipling. Lockwood's son, Rudyard, wrote a prophetic *Recessional* in the year of Victoria's Diamond Jubilee. Hauntingly, it predicted the end of Empire:

> Far-called our navies melt away;
> On dune and headland sinks the fire.
> Lo, all our pomp of yesterday
> Is one with Nineveh and Tyre!
> Judge of the nations, spare us yet,
> Lest we forget – lest we forget![1]

1897 found Amy Carmichael at Ootacamund in the Nilgiris Hills with her Indian helper, Saral. Her eye and heart were on a Kingdom that would never pass away. Ootacamund was one of the lofty hill stations to which Britons retreated when the outside air was like an oven, and on the plains every door was shut. Someone once wrote of this season, "the atmosphere within was only 104 degrees, as the thermometer bore witness, and heavy with the foul smell of badly-trimmed kerosene lamps; and this stench, combined with that of native tobacco, baked brick, and dried earth, sends the heart of many a strong man down to his boots, for it is the smell of the Great Indian Empire when she turns herself for six months into a house of torment."[2]

How nine hundred British civil servants and seventy thousand British soldiers ever managed to govern upwards of two-hundred-and-fifty million Indians is still a wonder to many. Without the relief of their hill stations at Darjeeling, Ootacamund, and supremely at Simla – which actually became the seat of Government for all of India for seven months of every year, they would probably never have survived.

Amy moved from Kotagiri to stay with a woman who would become her lifelong friend. Over the years, Mrs. Hopwood would open her doors to Amy and her ever-growing number of Indian girls. Here Amy continued with her language studies. Though not impressed with what she called the 'fashionable' Christianity of the British establishment around her, Amy rode in a bullock cart to the convention at Ootacamund, which was held especially for missionaries. They sang the Keswick hymns she loved so well, and she found herself listening intently to a thirty-six year-old missionary from the Tirunelveli area of Madras State, called Thomas Walker. He was eight years older than Amy. After the service, she was introduced to Thomas Walker in Ootacamund's Government Gardens, and they began to talk about her learning Tamil and how best it might be achieved. Amy told the gifted and experienced Walker that she would like to live in a mud hut among the people, learn Tamil properly, and disregard the comfort of a bungalow. Walker of Tirunelveli, whose biography Amy was to write one day, turned to her and insisted that she would not be able to stand such conditions for long. Amy decided she did not like him!

Mercifully, her first impressions did not last; for this man, known as *The Iyer* (an Indian term of respect and affection), was to become like her elder brother. He was one of her dearest friends and mentors, and arguably the best teacher she could ever have had. It is true that to teach is to touch a life forever: there are no more important people on the face of the earth than teachers, and their influence is incalculable. Walker himself, a master of Tamil, urged Amy to see that Tirunelveli would be a better place to learn the language than Bangalore. Was he right?

Amy returned to Bangalore from Ootacamund where, she wrote, "sheets of blue-grey rain blot out the trees in the compound." On the evening of Christmas Day 1896, she is writing, what she now calls, a *Scrap* letter from the town of Palmcottah in the Tirunelveli district. *The Iyer's* advice had been taken: she was to live in the Tirunelveli district of South India for the rest of her life. One imagines Amy at the end of Christmas day 1896, with thoughts of home and family in her heart, and her mind seeking to gather impressions of her new environment. As ever, her observant eye was not lazy: "After heavy monsoon rains, the colouring is very beautiful. Bright green paddy, darker green palms and trees, clear in the distance the purple of the hills, overall the blue sky. Then there are always such pretty native groupings. Photographs fall very flat as compared with the reality. I wish somebody would discover the art of photography in colours."

From the very beginning, Amy had liked Mrs. Walker; but now it was quite obvious that she had found an intellectual soul mate in her new teacher, Thomas Walker. Apart from his superb teaching of Tamil, she identified with his teaching of parables from the environment around him. "We begin our day by a humble drive, over roads made of mud-pools in some places, to the service in the little church in the heathen city of Tirunelveli . . . the road lies between paddy fields, shaded by fine old Banyan trees, and dotted all over the plain are thousands and thousands of Palmyra Palms." She then shares what she is learning from Thomas Walker's conversation on their daily journey: "He is a Tamil scholar, and reads the old Tamil poetry – he says there are many good things in it. You know that when missionaries are itinerating, they are often offered cocoa nut water – but does it keep it to itself? No, it gains it all by its roots – but does it keep it to itself? No, it gives it all out through its head! I need not add 'from this we learn,' but doesn't it make a capital illustration? Here is another: a little stream flows alongside the paddy fields. It is meant for the rice – but the weeds and grasses by the banks may share the water, too."

Amy continues to allow her readers to eavesdrop on the 'conversations-to-church,' as this teacher sent from God into her life shares his parables from the passing scenes. "One I liked very much," she writes, "was from the wide reaches of waving paddy plantlets, looking like miles of lovely grass as the wind blew over it, smoothing it level. If the green were stripped, what would you see? A great uneven field, all ridges and partitions. But let the rice grow up to the Harvest, and it is all one wide expanse of life and beauty. Don't let us go back to fundamentals in order to be 'one' – but let us go on to perfection." To Amy Carmichael and Thomas Walker, a paddy field was never just a paddy field!

One of her Eastern-picture-parables was a favourite of a famous Tamil missionary called Bishop Sargeant. He had pointed out that, "scattered about on these great fields are little plantations, around which a fence is thrown. It looks as though the fence was there to protect the trees. But no! The trees are only there for the sake of something else. Go closer, and you will see a tiny creeper turning round their trunks and branches. It is a Betel Nut, much prized by all the people. So, though the great world Governments and organisations seem of most importance – 'the real thing' – they really only exist for the sake of fulfilling God's purpose through the unseen church within." My, even a fence is not just a fence to Amy!

Her letter, begun on Christmas evening 1896, continues with her thoughts on New Year's evening 1897. "As I write, I can hear the tom-toms beating in the little heathen hamlet behind the house. It is Devil-worship-night. Every Tuesday and Friday, Mr. Walker says, all over the district this awful thing goes on. I can't tell you how real the sound is – it is like a sight and a sound mixed up. You seem to hear it, see it, and feel it all at once. Yesterday evening in the twilight I went alone to the little place and wandered up and down, just listening to the people and loving them. Most of them were in their huts, and no one could see me in the half-light. I could not do anything, and had not gone to try; but only to be near them on this last evening of the year. Saral met me as I was coming back, and we stood silently under the stars, longing – yes, just longing – for the coming of the King."

It was a great missionary heart beating under the stars on that last evening of 1896. Just as Christ was incarnated in order to reach us, He calls us to be incarnated to reach the world with His message. Amy could not do anything, particularly because of the language barrier between her and the people; but that barrier was soon to come down, and she would face, as few have done, the very powers of Hell. Her desire was not to Anglicise the Indian people, nor to imply that her civilisation was superior to theirs. She believed that the gospel of Christ is a truly liberating force for people in any civilisation, and the English need it every bit as much as the Indians do. Her incarnation to reach people with the gospel of Jesus Christ would prove to be awesome. Satan is a dirty fighter, and he uses unexpected people to do his work; but she, who was prepared in God's name to storm his battlements, was not to be left alone. "Sometimes," she wrote, "I wonder whether it is quite fair to keep to oneself all the loving things which happen, and which speak so very clearly of the nearness of the 'Living, personal, infectious God of Grace and Providence'. Often they are too much between my Lord and me for a *Scrap* letter."

Early in January 1897 she writes that she had received Dr. Moule's book *Prayer and Promises*, in which she had read about Hezekiah's letter from Sennacherib. "Commenting, Dr. Moule refers to the letters, among others, which come from 'possibly anonymous maligners', and advises that we should, as literally as possible, let Him see them. The immediate result will be something of that mental and spiritual calmness, which is the best receptacle for the whispers and messages of His answer, and the peace which passes all understanding comes and keeps." Amy then points out, "Today the post brought me an anonymous letter – or rather a couple of tracts, very nice ones – with a text written on the outside of the envelope. I looked it up, and felt the stab in the dark – for it was a text which implied something unkind and untrue, not about me only, but about my dear fellow workers; and, as it is anonymous, I can't defend them. I have often had letters to 'spread' before the Lord; but never before one of quite this kind. After the first minute of pain was over, I remembered how One very present help in trouble had been (though one did not know it) preparing one for this; and the rest in just knowing He knew, had known before it came, was very, very, sweet."

Is it not strange that the devil often uses another Christian to hurt a Christian most; and often it is when we are deeply involved in some advanced spiritual assault upon the enemy's kingdom? It has been pointed out that such action is akin to an army shooting its own wounded. The Lord had prepared Amy for the attempt to 'spike her guns' and, having been prepared, she was able to overcome the attack.

In those long months of language study, *The Iyer* kept Amy 'in the barracks'. Before the soldier would 'fight', training was necessary; so Amy was drilled by Thomas Walker in the Tamil language, including its proverbs, poetry and classics. Like Daniel, who was well schooled in the Chaldean language and literature before God led him into spiritual impact in that community, Amy had to face her second Tamil exams in February 1897. She felt very  inadequate, and wrote, "Never had a pupil such a teacher! But it is rather like a great Beethoven, wasting his time over a stupid little scale-strummer."

In February 1897, a change came in *The Iyer's* ministry for Christ. He and his wife felt they were being led by God to move from Palmcottah to the small town of Pannaivilai. Here, they felt, they should make a transition from administrative work to direct evangelistic work. *The Iyer* felt God was leading him to present the gospel to the people in the villages of that area. As Amy was staying with the Walkers at Palmcottah, studying and learning Tamil, Thomas Walker asked her to think and pray about joining them in this new outreach. He could see that Amy would be a wonderful ambassador for Christ amongst the women. As it turned out, Amy felt it would fit her like a glove and responded positively to the invitation.

In late February 1897, she travelled with the Walkers to visit Pannaivilai. On February 28th she wrote, "It is simply delicious being here . . . Oh, how I wish we could stay altogether. I like it so very much." She travelled by bullock-bandy, a springless, two-wheeled cart. She describes it as "the most tiring way of going about I ever came across." In July 1897, the Walkers and Amy moved to live in Pannaivilai. She reports that she passed her exams "badly"; but by August 1897 she was attempting to speak a little on her own.

"This has been a nice day," she writes on August 29th. "The Christian School boys, special chums of mine, dear little 'Royal Jewel', and various small fry gathered round." Amy then tells how they all went down to the lake, and had a sort of 'Children's Special Service' on a small scale. The harvest of the Children's Special Service Mission, planted in Harrogate in the late 1880's, was being reaped in India in the late 1890's. The seed had been carried a very long distance.

Through all those months of intensive language study, the evangelistic fire in Amy Carmichael's heart had never gone out. Her first *Scrap* letter of 1898 was red-hot! She refers to the times as "this Evil Age – astir all over the world. In the meantime, there is just one straight duty in front of us all – Fight!" She suggests to her friends, "The best way to really help and cheer up your missionary-comrades sometimes, is to send them *Missionary Books*!" She writes of how she finds reading such books an inspiration, as she struggles with "this beautiful, baffling language," and not being able to go out; or feeling "dull and flat and un-missionary altogether." She tells how, in such a situation, "you are certain to have tracts, and sermons, and nice, good little books in abundance." But, "take up Gilmour of Mongolia, or Harrington, or French, or any real, live battle-book you've got, and see if you feel braced up before you've been at it ten minutes. We don't want fiction in any shape or form, we haven't time for it. We don't always very much want sermons, but Hero lives – humdrum heroes though they be. Their stories any time – let's have them!"

She then gives her reading list: Gilmour of Mongolia, Harrington, Bishop French, Ragland of Tirunelveli, Henry Martyn of India, Burns of China, the Martyer Sisters of Fukien, Judson of Burma, Brainard of the North American Indians, and Bonar's *Life* of Robert Murray McCheyne. She calls them "a sort of standing dose of mental and spiritual quinine!"

Amy founded a women's band for the intended village outreach, and the Indians called them *The Starry Cluster*. As they set to work, the Amy who longed to fight a spiritual battle soon found that she had one of gigantic proportions on her hands. It would rock the religious, political, and missionary establishments around her, like she could never have imagined. She would become one of history's influential whistle-blowers. In fact, the battle began with jewels.

Walking Straight Into Her Heart

9 IT WAS 1898. Photographs were first taken with the use of artificial light. Sigmund Freud was set on proving the primacy of unconscious mechanisms; and, in 1898, he published an article entitled *The Physical Mechanism of Forgetting*. It was the first detailed examination of what became known as a 'Freudian slip'. Within the year, the man who wrote *Alice in Wonderland*, under the pseudonym Lewis Carroll, died; and the writing genius, C. S. Lewis, was born. In Kiev, Russia, Israel's future third Prime Minister, Golda Meir was born; and the man who was four times Britain's Prime Minister died of cancer, and was buried in Westminster Abbey. His name was William Gladstone. George Gershwin was born in America. He eventually bridged the gap between Tin Pan Alley and serious music. Gershwin was to compose light music, musicals, and make significant forays into a new form of classical repertoire.

Following the sinking of the Battleship *Maine* in Havana Harbour in April 1898, America declared war on Spain. The war ended with the Treaty of Paris in December 1898. As a result, Spain lost its control over the remains of its overseas Empire.

In 1898, Germany began passing Navy laws that identified the types and numbers of ships required for the German bid to become a world power. It was very much the personal aim of Kaiser Wilhelm II. The Germans saw England as their most dangerous naval enemy. In China, Tzu-Hsi, Dowager Empress of China, seized power and revoked reforms. John H. Nicholson and Sam Hill founded *Gideons International*, whose aim was to put the Word of God into the hands of the unconverted.

Under the crisp skies and dry heat of South India, Amy Carmichael was seeking to do the same with her group of women. However, towards the end of 1898, an issue of huge proportions arose in *The Starry Cluster*. It had to do with jewels. The question was not whether a Christian should wear jewellery; but was it appropriate, given the surrounding culture? Caste in India could be recognised by certain styles of jewels. Women were more or less sold to their husbands for so many rupees worth of jewels. Jewellery represented the wealth and status of a husband. The word 'jewels' embraced valuable old coins, weighty nose rings, bracelets set in precious gems, gold chains, ankle and finger rings. All over India, women were, in fact, walking safe-deposit boxes.

For a time Amy saw no problem in the matter, calling it 'a pretty custom', considering jewellery as part of the dress of women who worked with her. She had long opposed the 'foreignizing' trend of missionaries in India; and had taken to wearing a native sari herself, the dress of Indian women. In a small book about her early life, written in the 1940's for her grown-up children, Amy recounts an experience she had in Japan which convinced her that foreign clothes on a missionary could distract a listener from the all-important message being given, Consequently, she wore Indian dress from the very beginning of her work there. On the question of jewels, though, Amy began to see that the spirit of 1 Timothy 2:9 and 1 Peter 3:3-4 was being traduced for Christian women in India, by custom and culture, just as much as in the days of Paul and Peter. She prayed that if God wanted the question raised He would raise it among the Christian workers. And that is exactly what happened!

One day, as *The Starry Cluster* were travelling in connection with their work, a young husband, who was walking beside the bandy in which his wife was travelling, spoke to her about her jewels. He told her that jewels were inappropriate for one doing her kind of work. She took them off, and gave them to him. When the group of women got home to Pannaivilai, another worker, called Ponnammal, quietly took off her jewels. A third, called Sellamutthu, who had always slept at night with one hand on her necklaces, did the same.

Then the strife of tongues began. F. B. Meyer, the gifted Keswick Bible Teacher, arrived from England in February 1899, and addressed the problem as he taught the Scriptures. He simply did not know that he was lighting the touch paper of a very explosive issue. Women started to give their jewels to be sold, and the money was sent for Christian mission in China. Some returned their jewels to their families. The issue now began to swirl around Amy. In South Indian churches, sermons were preached against her. She was accused of 'dividing the church' and of 'teaching heresy'. The secular press sniffed out what was going on and, enlarging on the matter, they exaggerated it. Soon the Tirunelveli District was 'ablaze' with the issue. It was not to be the last time that Amy would defy custom.

The feeling among Ponnammal's relatives was that the issue would close the heart of Hindus to the Christian gospel. In fact, it had the very opposite effect on many Hindus. They deeply respected her decision, saying, "There are no boundaries set to her devotion." It also led to another, very practical, result: the fear of thieves was removed! *The Starry Cluster* could now journey in their bandy at night. As the years progressed, and hundreds of girls came under Amy's care, members of the Robber Caste who, according to Indian custom, were subsidised as an insurance agent against attack, agreed to help protect the girls. They said that, if the girls had been jewelled, they would not have done it.

How did this caring for girls begin for Amy? It began one morning in September 1898. A cry was heard on the verandah of the Mission bungalow at Pannaivilai. "Refuge! Refuge!" cried a 16 year-old girl's voice. What had happened? In the girl's village of Great Lake, close to Pannaivilai, there was a Mission school. No woman or child in the area had ever professed Christ as Saviour. The wife of the schoolmaster had given a Bible to a girl, and she had

become a secret believer. She told her brother that she loved the Lord Jesus, and he told the family. The family built a blazing bonfire and her father said to her, "If you mention Him again, you and your Bible will be thrown into the fire." One morning, as she lay beside her mother, the girl awoke. She was almost certain that she had been awakened by a hand that had touched her. A voice in her heart said, "Go!" So she stepped quietly over her sleeping relatives and, even though she had not been out of the house for three years, she ran down the street and crossed the stream to Pannaivilai. It was then that she cried, "Refuge!" on the steps of the verandah at the Mission bungalow. She had decided to follow the Lord Jesus, whatever the cost.

The cost proved to be enormous. Amy took the girl in, listened to her story, and determined to try and save her. First, her close relatives arrived and camped on the verandah. Her mother held long, heart-rending interviews with her. The emotional stress was tremendous, as her mother threw herself on the floor, beating her breast. Other family members kept up the pressure. The Revenue Inspector was called, and the Chief of Police was summoned. For days, the bungalow was literally under siege.

Why the opposition? It had to do with *caste*. In modern India, the more common term is *gati*. Castes can number many thousands of people, and are usually based on criteria relating to occupation or area of origin. In the West, people would understand it as a kind of trade-guild. Once born into a caste, an individual stays in it for life; although a person can be out-casted for a grave offence. Within Hinduism, for a long time caste has been the target of reforming groups; Ghandi himself tried to alter attitudes to 'untouchables'. In modern India today, attitudes to the whole caste system are changing.

In the Pannaivilai of 1899, though, no tolerance was being shown by a family to one of its members who wanted to become a Christian, because that family believed that, by doing so, she was breaking caste, which was to them a grave offence.

The girl belonged to the Goldsmith caste, whose members refine gold. The family tried all kinds of approaches to get the girl to change her mind. They threw 'magic dust' against her window at the Mission bungalow. Men of the Goldsmith caste stood under her window, waiting to seize her, and Thomas Walker had to nail the shutters closed. Soon forty men surrounded the house, waiting all day long. Three of them rushed at the door, but were stopped by an unseen hand. The family then made promises to the girl, saying they would not force her to marry, and they would let her go to church and worship God at home, as long as she would not break caste.

After some time, Thomas Walker brought matters to a head. He turned to the people besieging his home, and told them that they had had a fair chance to persuade the girl. He explained that she was free to go, if she wished. He turned to her and asked, "Do you chose to go?" "No," she replied. For days she kept repeating the words, *The Lord is my light and my salvation; whom shall I fear? The Lord is the strength of my life; of whom shall I be afraid?* (Psalm 27:1). Eventually, the siege was withdrawn; but the Mission school was burned down, and then the teacher's house.

The girl was taken into protection at a C.E.Z. Home in Palmcottah. She was eventually given the name 'Jewel of Victory' by the Christian poet, Krishna Pillai. The furore had barely subsided when another girl of the same Goldsmith caste arrived on the Pannaivilai verandah, clapped her hands, and cried "Refuge!" Again, day after day, the bungalow was under siege. Again, when the girl was determined to stay, she was moved for protection to Palmcottah. On June 13th 1900, in the first *Scrap* letter of the year, Amy described her baptism. For her, on that special day, the poet Krishna Pillai chose the name 'Jewel of Life'. Her name had formerly been 'Lady Child'.

The mode used for baptism was immersion, and Amy writes very movingly of its significance. First, she writes of asking Lady Child of the significance of the ordinance of baptism.

"Do you know what going down into the water means?" I asked her; "and she said quickly, 'Oh! It is a sign! I go down under the water – that is like dying, and I come up – that is like life! I say to the old things Go! I am dead to you! I am going to live to Jesus!' Mr. Walker preached about 'Refuge' from the 91st Psalm. Do you remember that when Lady Child came that morning, her final word – a breathless word – was "Refuge!" Then, we all went singing to the River.

I don't know whether I had ever told you that the Tamil idea of bathing is to stand about waist-deep, and dip down under the water. So baptism in this way is the most natural thing to them. There is nothing foreign or extraordinary in it, and they see the symbolic meaning at once. So, when Lady Child went into the river, following Mr. Walker who is like a father to her, she was not the least self-conscious; but as simply as a child she stood there, waiting, while we sang *Jesus is my Life, my Life is Jesus*. She then came back, 'Jewel of Life', with such a glad look on her face. It brought the tears to one's eyes – strangely made beings are we!

. . . You remember she knew nothing, had not even heard of Jesus, before she came. The more we see of the tremendous odds there are against any soul, especially any girl soul coming out, the more marvellous it seems that, to this one – so dark, so ignorant, so unknowing what she was choosing – there should have been given a gift so glorious: the 'Jewel of Life'."

And Amy herself: how did she feel under all this strain? She noted on January 13th 1900,

"He saw a Hand they could not see,
Which beckoned him away.
He heard a voice they could not hear,
Which would not let him stay!

This day, this hour, eight years ago, my marching orders came. Even now as I write, the solemnity of that hour is upon me. There is something most awfully resistless in Royal Orders. There is only one thing to be done – obey.

Oh, one grows more and more intensely Missionary every year! Knowing for certain that our God will keep His Word to those who are at home, one can only rejoice with all one's heart and soul that, should the Captain call the Battle Roll tonight, one may answer 'Present' still."

The Battle Roll was soon to be called to the greatest spiritual battle of Amy Carmichael's life, and she was to be found 'present', so very present.

The Starry Cluster continued their Christian work; now aided by tents, including a small one for Thomas Walker, and a 12′ x 12′ two-sided tent for the women missionaries. (In fact, for almost seven years, Amy worked in this itinerant ministry in the towns and villages of Tirunelveli.) After the village of Great Lake was closed to gospel work, a new door opened in a village called 'Uncrowned King', seven miles away. A little girl, on the outskirts of the crowd at an open-air service in her village, heard an Indian Christian speak of Christ 'turning him from a lion into a lamb'. The child had a bad temper, and longed to have it changed, so she was touched by what the man said. The child's name was Arulai, and her story is told in Amy Carmichael's book *Ploughed Under*. For over 40 years, until her death, Arulai was to be a close and valued friend of Amy Carmichael, and a woman who became a truly great Christian.

In 1900, a move was made from Pannaivilai to the village of Dohnavur, because it was a suitable place for Thomas Walker to teach a class of Divinity Students of the Church Missionary Society. They met in the church building in the village. The plan was to stay for only a few months. All of Amy's belongings remained at Pannaivilai. Dohnavur had been established in 1827 by an outstanding Prussian missionary and visionary, called C. T. E. Rhenius. The village was named after a Count Dohna, who had sent money for persecuted Christians at one stage in Charles Rhenius' ministry. His money had financed the church building in the village. Persecution of Christians had reached such a stage that 'Villages of Refuge' were necessary. Dohnavur was one of the Villages of Refuge, and soon it was awesomely to live up to its name.

On March 4th 1901, *The Starry Cluster* left Dohnavur to return to the village of Pannaivilai, arriving on the evening of March 6th. Something happened that evening, which was to change the course of Amy Carmichael's life. Indisputably, it was of God. Amy firmly believed that an angel had come to the temple in Great Lake that night, taken a little seven-year-old child called Preena by the hand, and led her out across the same stream that Jewel of Victory had crossed. A Christian woman found her in the woods near the village of Pannaivilai, "a very small and desolate mite with tumbled hair and troubled eyes." Because it was late, the Christian woman took Preena to her home for the night, fully intending to return her to the temple the next day. The little mite kept insisting, though, that she wanted to go to the one she called 'the child-catching *amma*' (mother).

Early in the morning, Amy was having tea on the verandah at the bungalow at Pannaivilai, when she saw the Christian woman coming with a little girl. The child ran straight to Amy, climbed into her lap and said, "My name is Pearl-eyes," and announced that she had come to stay, always. Amy kissed the little mite, and later wrote, "The little thing walked straight into our hearts, and we felt we would risk anything to keep her." In truth, she did risk everything to keep Preena, and was to learn things from her that "darkened the sunlight." Amy's life would never be the same again.

Alice In Underland

10   IT WAS 1905. Hard-packed snow lay on the streets
of St. Petersburg, as loyal strikers marched through
the city to appeal to Tsar Nicholas II for better
conditions. Led by a youthful priest called Father George Gapon,
they headed for the Winter Palace where Gapon hoped to deliver a
petition to the Tsar. The priest carried a cross; others marching behind
him carried icons, flags, and the Tsar's portrait. Lines of infantry,
backed by Cossacks, blocked the way. Without warning, at a distance
of only thirty yards, the troops opened fire on men, women, and
children. More than five hundred died, many others were wounded.
Any illusion that the Tsar and the people were one was shattered
that day.

In March 1905, Theodore Roosevelt was inaugurated for his first
full term of office as United States President since succeeding the
assassinated William McKinley in 1901. In April 1905, intelligence
tests (the bane of children's lives) were invented by the French
Psychologist, Alfred Binet. He aimed to measure intelligence rather
than knowledge. In Britain, a bill to give women the vote was 'talked
out' by Members of Parliament at Westminster. To his eternal shame,
one MP audaciously stated that giving women the vote "would not
be safe," and that "men and women differed in mental equipment,

with women having little sense of proportions." Aspirin went on sale in Britain for the first time in 1905; no doubt women needed it, to help them put up with such prejudiced men!

In April, more than ten thousand people were feared dead in an earthquake which rocked the North East Indian province of Lahore. At Simla, Lady Curzon, wife of the Viceroy, had a close escape from death when a chimney crashed into the room in which she was sleeping. Indeed, 1905 was quite a year for the Curzon family. In August, Lord Curzon resigned, because of a quarrel he had with the British Government about the reorganisation of the Indian Army. Curzon, who oversaw the restoration of the Taj Mahal, once admitted that British rule in India "may be good for us; but it is neither equally nor altogether good for them."

And Amy? 1905 found her continuing to spread the good news of the gospel that was equally good for everyone. But there was a heartache. A jewel of a child was dying. When she had come to Dohnavur Amy had named her Indraneela, meaning Sapphire. Now Amy was being called upon to give her up to the Lord; so it was a heart-rending moment when the little one broke the silence with one little cry, "Amma!" Then, as Amy put it, "the Angel came, so gently touched her that she slept, and woke to the music of Heaven."

I have stood at the ruins of the church building in Anwoth, Scotland, where Samuel Rutherford was minister in the seventeenth century, and reflected on the qualities of that great Professor of Divinity at St. Andrew's University, who eventually died in prison for his faith. I have mused by his grave in St. Andrew's, while reading the words on his gravestone:

> His learning justly raised his fame,
> True godliness adorned his name.
> He did converse with things above,
> Acquainted with Emmanuel's love.

Rutherford was a man with a tender heart; and it was to his writings that Amy Carmichael turned for comfort when little

Indraneela died. She found great consolation in the following words, which I have slightly abridged to relate to twentieth century eyes:

"You have lost a child," he wrote. "Nay, she is not lost to you, who is found to Christ; she is not sent away but only sent before, like unto a star which, going out of our sight, doth not die and vanish, but shineth in another hemisphere: you see her not, yet she doth shine in another country. If her glass was but a short hour, what she wanteth of time that she hath gotten of Eternity: and you have to rejoice that you have now some treasure laid up in Heaven . . . Your daughter was a part of yourself, and you, being as it were cut and halved, will indeed be grieved; but you have to rejoice that when a part of you is on earth, a greater part of you is glorified in Heaven. *There is less of you out of Heaven* (now) *that the child is there.*"

It was January 6th 1905. As Amy gathered Indraneela's things together, folding them to put them away, she decided that at Dohnavur the sixth day of the month would be kept as 'a day of prayer for all imperilled children, wherever they may be.' It still is.

We left Amy with Preena (Pearl Eyes) on the verandah of the Mission bungalow at Pannaivilai. What had happened in the interval? Thomas Walker and the Tamil pastor felt that the best course of action was to verify her story, so a messenger was sent to Great Lake. Soon some of the Temple Women arrived, and Preena said to them and to the large crowd that had gathered, "I won't go with them!" And little wonder, for when on a former occasion Preena had escaped to her mother's home from the Temple Women's house, the Temple Women followed her, and her mother gave her back to them. They branded her hands with hot irons as a punishment for attempting to escape. So Preena stayed, and she became the first of a family of Temple children that were to become legendary.

From Preena Amy learnt things that indeed, for her and those who supported her, 'darkened the sunlight.' Eventually, the Indian Government, which was set up on Independence, passed a law which made it illegal to dedicate young children to a god.

The first woman to sit in an Indian Legislature, Dr. Mutthulaksmi Reddi, a Madras Physician who was against the practice, stated that "innocent children are made victims, and are prepared for an immoral life by a course of training from their early days. The Temple and the illiterate Hindu public are responsible for developing a kind of mentality in those children, which makes them, when they grow to be women, through an immoral, unholy and anti-social act . . . as a hereditary right and a caste dharma (duty)." In *Young India*, October 6th 1927, Mahatma Gandhi, stated, "There are, I am sorry to say, many Temples in our midst in this country which are no better than brothels."

The courage of the Indian Government to ban the practice is to be highly commended; but in the India of the early twentieth century it took incredible courage to honour the facts, challenge the practice, and protect the victims. This extraordinary work, involving a full frontal attack on the horrendous practice, was taken on by no less than Amy Wilson-Carmichael. But let no one, anywhere, underestimate the price that she paid.

After Preena's arrival, Amy continued in her itinerary work with *The Starry Cluster*, and by June 1901 she was Amma to four more children. They were not Temple children, but they all needed help. By day as she travelled, she kept looking out for Temple children. At night, she returned to little Preena and the other children at Dohnavur. In fact, it took a three-year search before Amy could find the sources from which the Temple procured infants and children. Preena talked freely about what went on, and what she had personally experienced. The more she talked, the more Amy's heart, mind, soul and body were fired-up to do something about the problem. The truth was that, although she maintained a happy exterior for Preena's sake, Amy wept in secret at what she had told her. It was almost unbearable for her, as slowly and carefully she started to build up the facts. She wrote to missionaries, but drew a blank. There were some who even hinted that she was imagining things. The Indian Civil Service knew something, but could prove nothing; and on all points, of course, the Raj maintained 'religious neutrality.' Amy had started to 'rock the boat', and she described it as 'a bitter time', even calling herself 'Alice in Underland'.

On one occasion, Amy and her friend, Ponnammal, slept in a cow shed. "The cow was away," Amy explained. As they lay on the manure-covered dirt floor, they heard a quarrel going on in the house. "Three daughters? Too many," said a voice. "Get rid of one." A woman started to sob. "Give one to the Temple," said the voice. "Is it not a worthy deed?"

Of course, there were reverent Hindus who vigorously opposed the degrading practices that had crept into their religion. One newspaper clipping sent to Amy stated, "The Council of Hindu Reformers supports the movement to better the condition of unprotected children in general . . . and to protect girls and young women from being dedicated to Temples." But Amy knew that she needed to find evidence to prove her case. Slowly, and with ever deepening sadness, she discovered the horrendous evidence.

Soon Amy was glad that God had said "No" to her childhood prayer in Millisle for blue eyes. One night she disguised herself by staining her hands and face with coffee and, dressed in a sari, she got right past the priests. Eventually she got to the inner shrine and then entered a larger room where ten little girls, all aged between four and six, stood in line, waiting. Dressed in silk saris and sparkling with jewels, they were perfumed and wore flowers in their hair, but their eyes were filled with fear. A door opened, weird music burst from behind the door, and a priest led them in. Amy did not need to be told what it was all about. But how was she to tell the world and the authorities that the horrors were real, and not imagined?

Painstakingly, that is exactly what she did. In her book *Things as They Are* she attempted to put the horrors into words. Because of the disturbance her book was causing, a committee of Christians met in India to ask that she be sent back to England. Amy was now rocking the Christian boat; never to speak of the Hindu boat, and even the ship-of-State!

I have in my hand at this very moment a photocopy of Amy's typed report of the facts that she eventually unearthed in her travels. It makes my blood run cold. It starts with the story of Preena, and what Amy learned from her. It tells of these children being taught to dance, and their fingers being bent right back to make them supple. The stories which the children were told by an 'elder brother' were unclean stories; and when Preena had refused to listen to them she was punished. "She once all but told of something done to other children before the tali (jewel) was given to them, but stopped." The tali, which hung around a child's neck, was the symbol of that child being married to a god. Said Amy, "It was what she did not say, rather than what she said, that drove me to do something to save children like Muttachi (Preena's Tamil name)."

In what she calls, "A Personal Note as to how I learned something of the under-life of the people," Amy writes,

"It was soon evident that if children were ever to be saved I must learn more of the conditions prevailing among the Temple people. At first I tried to find these things out by asking any who might be supposed to know, English or Indian. But I learnt nothing. I found, too, that even the modified English life, lived with English fellow missionaries, prevented my getting at the core of anything. So I often left them and went away alone with one or two Indian women and lived almost like a Tamil, in Madams by the roadside, or in towns, or with a married convert who lived in a town. At once it was as if that invisible film of feeling went – I was sensible of being allowed *in*. Often I went to night festivals, and sometimes I was carried with a stream of chattering women into the inner parts of the Temple and had in various other ways opportunities afforded by this sordid life for hearing things not usually discussed in the presence of foreigners. Once in a roadside eating-house, where we were spending the evening, the people as they came in offered me the salutation they offer to a Brahman widow on pilgrimage. I found they had mistaken me for one. Perhaps this explains why they talked so freely. But even where they made no mistake as to my nationality they took little notice of me. In the Madams connected with Temples, where alms are given daily to the poor, it is sometimes usual for the garland-makers to sit on the floor until late evening, making the garlands for the next day's worship. Sometimes we stayed in the room next to the one where the idol was, and in the evenings sat with the garland-makers on the floor in the front of the idol, and heard many things concerning the life of the town. In such ways the following things were learned . . ."

She learned that all over the area there were people on the look-out for children suitable for Temple service. Often they were, Amy points out, "Ordinary people, the village barber for example, or the bazaar-keeper, who, without going out of his way to do it, passes to the nearest Temple woman any information which comes to him as to a likely child." She found that anybody, "man or woman, who has any desire for merit or money, may at any time find and take a child to a Temple house; many informally help in this way." The Temple Women themselves and their servants, she discovered, went about making friends with all and sundry. There was "no systematic search, so far as I know; everything is haphazard and 'anyhow' as to arrangements, but it is very effective." She points out: "in fifteen years' effort to find and save these children, I cannot recall one instance where we were first on the field as far as a child suitable for the Temple was concerned. Hospitals, festivals, markets, even back streets or remote country villages, all seemed to be under observation."

Amy envisages "the kind of child considered suitable." She states,

"The fatherless child of good birth comes first, I think, in the list of children in danger. The family will usually adopt the other children, but the baby girl with all the future expenses involved is too much. Often the mother is told she must give this last little one to the Temple. Especially if it is born after the father's death, it is very likely to be devoted. The inducement to the mother is the merit to be thereby acquired: merit sufficient to cancel the sin which accounts for her widowhood. Or there will be an appeal to her affections: 'You have tasted the bitterness of widowhood. Therefore, should you not so arrange matters for your child that she shall never be a widow?' This is a tremendously strong argument, and often prevails."

Then come the orphan child left with relatives, and the child of a mixed marriage."

A "mixed marriage" does not necessarily mean the marriage of two people of different race, but often between people of different caste. Amy found that some children were 'vowed', or 'dedicated', in order to avert disaster. She continues with her list:

"In some castes and families, it is the custom to give one child in each generation. Such a child is usually chosen for special brightness of mind, as it is necessary she should be mentally active. Then there are child-widows and the illegitimate child, of which there are two kinds: the children of women who have deliberately chosen an evil life, and the children of virtuous widows forced into sin. Riverbanks are the great places of meeting between Temple Women and their scouts and these young widows and lately-widowed women. A woman will sit on the bank quietly watching, or mingle with the women as they bathe or clean their vessels or wash their garments. She listens to the talk, learns the gossip of the village, and acts accordingly."

Amy outlines the special training of the Temple child.

"Often she is sent to school; at about eight or nine the special training begins. This consists in the finger massage mentioned before, and in dancing and poetry lessons. About this time too begins the systematic telling of vile stories. The child has to listen. If, as sometimes happens, she is repelled by them, and with a child's outspokenness says so, this natural instinct is dealt with – she is coaxed and cajoled into listening or laughed at for her silliness. An Indian child can stand anything better than being laughed at. She generally gives in at this point. If she does not, there are ways of compelling her. I do not think Temple Women are by nature cruel, they are an easy-going set; but if a child crosses the will of those who have set their minds on defiling her mind, she need look for no pity. Once conquered, the child may have a pleasant time. It is quite possible that the other preparation, which a little later is sure to begin, will include nothing cruel. But it will almost complete her mental demoralisation. It is thus that she is prepared for her 'marriage'."

Amy proceeds to graphically describe the ceremony of 'a marriage to a god', the appearance of Temple-houses, and the position of Temple Women in the thoughts of the people. In fact, this turns out to be contradictory, for they are held both in honour and in scorn. The Tamil name for a Temple Woman is Devadasi, in shortened form it is Dasi. Deva means 'god', and dasi means 'servant'. Devadasi means, therefore, 'Servant of god.' "All that is implicit in the fact that an honoured name is theirs," writes Amy, "– which name no virtuous woman would bear – expresses exactly, I think, the thought of the people about them. They are honoured, and they are despised."

"I have often seen the honour. The best places in festivals are kept for them, apart from requiring front places for service on the gods. They are never hustled about as others are in a crowd: a way is made for them wherever they wish to go. Even a child (from the Temple house), being recognised by her probably neat and pretty dress and general air, seems to be safe anywhere. I have seen such a one far from her home, alone except for a child attendant, in a big town on a festival evening, treated kindly and even politely by the people. She was perfectly safe among them: it was 'lucky' to see her. Sometimes I have come across a child alone in a houseful of men at midnight, singing to them, the old grandfather with his arm round her, as if she were his grandchild.

And I have seen the scorn. The effect of the shock of awakening to its existence is sometimes very visible on the child or girl to whom life up till that moment had been happy enough. I have seen such a child cry her heart out over the first hard word that told her what she had never known before. I have seen a girl, stolen away from her home as a baby, crushed to the dust as the word trampled over her.

The sense of this double treatment being unjust, never seems to trouble the Hindu, and he expresses himself frankly in his proverbs, unbothered by the incongruity of things. If he meets a widow in the morning, he is concerned: if a dasi, he is charmed. The one brings bad luck, the other good. For many it was 'lucky' to see a Temple Woman: to see her was to be 'charmed'. *When the dasi's mother dies, the drums will beat. When the dasi dies, no drums*, is a proverb that sums up the position of the Temple woman. Those who want to win her favour make great lamentation over her mother's death. When nothing is to be got from her, who cares for her?"

Amy records the duties and pay of the Temple Women, and their common practice of adopting the children who have been taken into the Temples. As one reads her notes, the sense of the immensity of the task of rescuing children from such a system is overwhelming. How did she ever get the courage to pluck so many children from the jaws of this giant of abuse and evil? The answer is that she yielded herself to the hands of the Vinedresser. Jesus said, *I am the true Vine, and my Father is the Vinedresser* (John 15:1). He spoke of His people as being branches in the Vine. The vine is certainly a fruit-tree, yet it cannot stand upright like other fruit-trees. Its branches are very pliant, so it requires a skilful hand to guide them along the trellises. If there is to be good, fruit producing, branch-life, then we must yield to the loving hands of the Vinedresser. We may sincerely desire to grow a certain way, but our purposes and sense of direction can be far different from what the Vinedresser wants. He may twist us, fasten us, and nail us in a certain place much against our will, but what is the result? The result is luscious grapes. If we yield to the Vinedresser, we too will be a blessing beyond our expectations.

Slowly the Vinedresser began to fasten Amy to the village of Dohnavur. It was quite a fastening, for here was a woman whose way of moving, according to an older lady of *The Starry Cluster*, called Blessing, was neither walking nor running, but 'flying'. The wild-bird child in Amy was constantly active! For example, 1902 found her at Travancore, speaking with Thomas Walker at the annual convention of the Reformed Syrian Church, attended by as many as twenty thousand people. Amy could have been a huge success as a speaker, but as her life moved on she consistently refused invitations to work outside the ministry to which God was now clearly calling her. As calls started to come to her from all over South India, she asked, "Could it be right to turn from so much that might be of profit, and become just nurse maids?" As she read of Christ washing His disciples feet, Amy was reassured that by no means was she wasting any of the gifts the Lord had given her.

On March 1st 1904, Amy made a note "A pastor, at work in North Tirunelveli, saw in the street of the village where he was working, Temple Women and children, at night. He was stirred by the sight, began to enquire into the matter of adoption of children, and, hearing of a baby about to be adopted, appealed to the Superintendent of Police who happened to be in the neighbourhood. The result was that the child was saved and sent to me. The little thirteen-day-old child was the very first Temple-baby to be rescued, and was called Amethyst by Preena, who was allowed to name her. She chose the name from Revelation 21:20."

By June 1904, Amy had seventeen children and six babies under her care, preserved from entering the Temple. By now she was working day and night at full stretch, as mother, doctor and nurse, under very restricted facilities. Some of the children desperately needed breast-feeding, but such a practice was not done in the village. When eventually one woman consented to breast feed one of Amy's babies in order to save its life, her husband killed her by slow arsenic poisoning. He believed she deserved it because she had sinned against caste.

Amy lists story after story of the work of trying to save these children. The stress and pressure of her work is nowhere more powerfully stated than in the following:

"On September 10th 1904 a child was brought to us whom we had been tracking quietly for some months. Her mother had been lately widowed, and hearing her elder brother plotting the sale of the child to a Temple in Travancore she had tried to drown her as it was the only way she knew of saving her from the life. This failed, and the brothers then gave the mother some sort of mind-destroying drug. She lost her reason and wandered about with the child. One morning before she was awake, someone (presumably under the brother's direction) stole the child, then eighteen months old, from her side, and passed it from hand to hand till it reached the woman known to one of the people with whom we were in touch. She let us know at once about it, and we sent off to try to get it. The woman entrusted with the sale had just reached the border when our messenger overtook her and we got the child. For weeks after it came to us the sight of water sent it into a panic of terror. The mother disappeared, and we heard nothing more of her.

About this time I heard of a child in the hospital at Tuticorin, whose mother had died in hospital, and whom the Temple Women of that town were trying to get. I wired to the Collector for leave to get it, and when leave was granted sent for it. My worker returned after four days' vain endeavour to get it. As soon as it was known we were after it, hindrances were put in the way; the telegram which she showed had no affect except to cause her to be politely treated. She was kept first at the Tahsildar's court, then at the hospital, hour after hour during the whole of three days, waiting while other business was discussed. When at last she was called before the Tahsildar, she was told to give an account of our work, and then told to come next day for the child. When she went, the child was dead. A nurse she knew in the hospital told her it had been kept, with hardly any food, in a room in which a woman had died, where the smell was sure to kill it. Everyone was very polite and concerned that all her trouble had been in vain."

It was a great moment for Amy when, in November 1904, Thomas Walker returned from his year's furlough with her mother, Mrs. David Carmichael. Mrs. Walker was unable to return to Dohnavur because of ill health, but *The Iyer* escorted Mrs. Carmichael to Dohnavur. A nursery had been built at Dohnavur during the year, and the money for it had come in direct answer to prayer. Amy had gone for a walk and prayed as she walked, adding the sums in her head and figuring out the cost of the bricks. When she returned, she found that her mail had arrived and in it was a cheque for the very amount she had just decided on! She purchased the field, and immediately received another gift earmarked 'for the nursery'. She had told no one of the need. It was the largest sum Amy had yet received. As Mrs. Carmichael settled in, she wrote to a friend at home, "In this large family of over 30, ranging in age from 34 years to a babe of nine months, I have not seen an angry look, or heard an impatient word. A set of more loving, unselfish women and girls and children could not easily be found."

Soon, though, a great sadness came to Dohnavur. An epidemic struck, and two babies died; one of them was Amethyst. Now only one baby was left, and it was Indraneela. Her death, on January 6th 1905, as described at the beginning of this chapter, was devastating for Amy. "She was a child of kingly race, one of the royal races of India; every dainty way and pretty gesture showed it. There was something very noble about her. She was our best." The Lord had taken Indraneela away, and Amy had to yield her up. She wrote:

Dear little feet, so eager to be walking,
But never walked in any grieving way.
Dear little mouth, so eager to be talking,
But never hurt with words it cannot say.
Dear little hands, outstretched in eager welcome;
Dear little head that close against me lay –
Father, to Thee I give my Indraneela,
Thou wilt take care of her until That Day.

So, for the rest of her life, Amy always kept the 6th day of the month as a day of prayer for all imperilled children, wherever they might be.

In the midst of all Amy's sadness in 1905, God was leading her through the waters and flame of her trials (see Isaiah 43:2). The work she was doing locally began to move slowly towards a national dimension. On May 20th 1905, she wrote a letter from *Limond House*, Ootacammund in the Nilgiris Hills. The broken-hearted Amy lifted her eyes away beyond her immediate circumstances to the vast subcontinent in which God had placed her; and the light of guidance was dawning upon her, that what she was doing had vast repercussions. In this chapter, we have looked at some of the facts she collected regarding the Temple children; but here, in her own words, the seed-thought is expressed for what lay ahead:

"We are hoping to gather facts concerning the Temple children matter during the next year, and then, probably through the Missionary body of South India, approach Government upon the subject . . . if only the facts can be brought to light, something will surely be done. The difficulty is to get the facts: facts of the sort which will compel action on the part of the Government. The law as it stands is inadequate to cope with this trade in children. We realise that it will be difficult to frame the law, that its purpose cannot be evaded; but when one sees so many thoughtful men and women, some of them Government Officials, tackling the question, one feels as if the day when right will be done may not be so very far distant. I have begun with this because I want your prayers. *The subject is National, not just Missionary, in its bearing.*"

Amy the missionary was also on her way to becoming a social reformer, to the huge benefit of the nation she loved, and of which she had become a part.

The Fire That Could Not Injure

11   IT WAS 1906. The Olympic Games were back in Athens after around 2,600 years. Russia's first elected Parliament, the Duma, opened; and in San Francisco a major earthquake killed at least one thousand people. The city's industrial areas and financial district were wiped out. The thirty-second earth tremor caused an estimated $200 million worth of damage. In London, the Suffragettes were causing mayhem in rowdy demonstrations during the opening session of Parliament. Around the same time, the police, due to licensing laws requiring 'no undue noise', ordered many London buses off the road. In 1906, for the very first time, a picture was transmitted by telegraph over more than one thousand miles by a German professor. Ominously the first German submarine U1 entered service. Amy Carmichael would have been delighted to learn that in France Gabriel Lippman had presented a new method of colour photography to the Academie des Sciences; for she had longed for someone to discover it.

In June 1906, though, Amy was writing of discoveries to sicken the heart: "The further we go in our investigations, the more appalling the traffic in little children seems. All over the extreme South and for four or five hundred miles North we knew it existed and flourished undetected. But I was not prepared to find it as widespread and if possible more cruelly conducted in Nizami's dominions, in Berar, and in certain parts of the Bombay Presidency. On the West Coast, moreover, they have the very thing we have in the South, and a band of workers is trying to deal with it at Poona."

The care of the babies who had been saved was a huge task for Amy and her helpers. The Dohnavur family had been divided, as a new nursery had been opened at Neyyoor: a Medical Mission Station a long day's journey from Dohnavur. Ponnammal (known as 'Golden'), the women's itinerary leader, was in charge of the babies. There, the medical missionaries were very kind to Dohnavur babies, and the Tamil helpers too. The problems they faced are epitomised in the following letter, written by Amy on October 8th 1906:

"I posted my last letter on a sorrowful day: the baby we were anxious about died. The milk seller deceived Ponnammal (Golden), who is in charge of the Neyyoor Nursery. The milk was poured into a brass vessel, the inner lining of which had worn out. Metallic poison defies boiling. The little baby had only one bottle, but it killed her. She had been with us from her birth, and was one of the few perfectly healthy babies we have had. She had never once been ill, and was a constant little joy to us all. After drinking her milk that morning, she lay playing and talking to herself, until the poison began to work, and the change in the little face startled Ponnammal, who from that moment knew there was no hope."

Amy then writes of another child who had been reclaimed by her mother:

"She was such a dear little girl with such a pretty little face and gentle manners, we loved her before we knew how very loveable she was. We called her Lala . . . on May 22nd little Lala was given to us. On June 22nd she was taken from us. On July 13th she was with Jesus.

As the little one lay dying, we heard afterwards, she called her mother and told her that she saw three people in shining white, and she said, 'I am going to Jesus'. Her heathen mother did not understand, and told a Christian neighbour about it. Lala was such a short time with us that we feared she had understood very little; but I think we have all learned to expect more since we heard how, after her return home, she used to pray morning and evening to Jesus, and she told the people she was His little child. Think of that dear little one dying . . . but comforted in that last hour by what surely was a vision of Angels, the Shining Ones the pilgrims saw by the riverside. Oh, we can trust the Good Shepherd to take care of His little lambs."

Throughout her life and writing Amy Carmichael's belief in angels and their ministry was deep and real. This belief was of paramount comfort to her and is caught beautifully in her poem *Lift up thy heart*:

The child lay dying, and I looked and saw
Through the open nursery window, pale blue hills
In quiet folds beyond the garden wall.
  And as I looked, I thought: If I could see
  God's angels standing on those blue hillsides,
  With faces turned in welcome towards the child,
  And hands outstretched to take her, would I toil
  So hard to keep her from them? Would I not
  Loose her and let her go? And then this song awoke:

If we could see all the surrounding spaces,
Blue hills or gardens, or the common street,
Bright with the heavenly people's welcoming faces,
  Say, would we still entreat
  In desperate prayer
  For sojourn in the broken house of clay?
  Oh, could we hear the music in the air,
  Would we then toil or pray
  For long imprisonment?

If we could see the quickened powers awaken,
Each from its sheath, like buds newborn on earth,
And the free spirit, wind-swept, overtaken
  By racing waves of mirth,

Jubilant spray,
Breast the great breakers of its happiness,
Would we not rise up then and quietly say,
'My God, I acquiesce;
Yea, I am well content.'

Did Amy buckle under all the stress? Did she lose a Christian perspective in the face of the heartbreaking tasks she had to confront every day? Let her own words answer that question: "So, even here and even now, the joys outweigh the troubles; and I think when we reach 'the Laughing Side of Life', as old Samuel Rutherford called it, we shall wonder why we were not always singing in the ways of the Lord." In the light of Amy's circumstances, those are remarkable words.

The overall task before Amy was to bring down the evil trade in little children. It was never far away from her mind and heart. In June 1906, she wrote:

"The week before last I met a medical worker who for some time lived in a house next door, or very near, a Temple house in a certain Indian city. She used to be awakened at 3.00 in the morning by the agonised screams of children. She enquired, and was told that the woman in charge was only beating them. Something far worse was being done. That woman finds it worth her while to buy babies at 10 rupees (13 shillings and four pence) each, and to care for them until they are nine years old. They more than repay the expenditure. One's very soul is sickened as one hears more and more of the working of the system which, so far as I know, is unique even among Eastern nations for uttermost cruelty."

Amy refers to Mrs. Thomas Walker's joyful return to Dohnavur, and her own Mother's sorrowful departure, as the two outstanding domestic events of the year 1906. "Welcomes," she states "are delightful things; but goodbyes are perfectly dreadful." As she refers to the future, she feels she had better leave it: "it may never come – for the Lord Jesus may come. Oh, wouldn't that be good." Here was a Christian who was not cowering in shame at the thought of

Christ coming, but who was positively glorying in the very thought of it.

The year 1906 had a frightening sting in its tail. On Christmas Day, Amy was awakened long before dawn by an anxious voice at her bedside. It was the mother of one of the Divinity students. Her daughter had cholera. The disease was stalking Dohnavur village. Amy writes, "We sent for the nearest Government apothecary, and he had 'fever'. We learned to diagnose such fever easily. We gave it another name, 'Funk', so we had to work on alone."

Mercifully, Amy had access to medicine and so many lives were saved, but many died. (Dr. Nancy Robbins, who knew Amy personally when she worked at Dohnavur, and saw Amy every day for the last two-three years of her life, has told this author that the 'medicine' to which Amy had access was potassium permanganate. Amy administered it in very small doses in large quantities of water – it was the water that was the lifesaver, and the symbiotic action of prayer! It had, of course, the psychological benefit of being cared for and given hope. Dr. Robbins adds, "I don't think anyone else has had such success with this non-medicine!") Eight out of twelve people were taken by cholera in the house of Putatan, the village barber. Amy writes of the deaths of two children during the epidemic:

"The little lad passed away that night. As he lay dying, a little girl played on the doorstep and salaamed with a bright smile as we passed out. Next day she had it, in exactly the same desperately violent form. Within a few hours, she was unrecognisably changed. The dear little child's face was the face of a haggard old woman. The terror of death was upon her, and she clung to me with both her little hands, as it came nearer and nearer. It was almost as if she saw it, and shrank back from its touch. Her poor mother in agony cried to me to pray that she might pass painlessly. I had been praying all the time, but as the child screamed in terror that was terrible to see I prayed aloud, and suddenly the little form lay still. From that moment there was not a struggle; we hardly knew when she left us. "Oh, Amma, I believe in your God now," said the poor mother. "See, she is at peace! He was listening. I believe in Him now." Words spoken at such a time don't always mean much, but I did hope for that mother. The village barber, Putatan, after all he had been through, arrived at church and avowed himself a worshipper of the True God. 'Our gods forsook us', he said. 'They were worth just nothing to us in our extremity.'"

Despite the heartbreaks, the spiritual work of helping to build Christ's Kingdom continued. A truth that is absolute in any generation continued to be one of Amy's guiding stars through all her difficulties. It is caught perfectly in a statement she quotes, which is found on the gateway of Milan Cathderal: *"All that pleases is but for a moment. All that troubles is but for a moment. Nothing is important but that which is eternal."*

Baptisms were moments of immense encouragement and inspiration for Amy. As Easter 1907 approached, her description of the baptism of six children reflects her deep feelings.

"We had thought of Easter Sunday, but the Sunday before suited better. There was an extra special joy in its happening on that day, the day when the light made a glory around the Man of Sorrows. As we went down to the waterside, the children sang over and over again, Hosanna! Hosanna! Hosanna! We met in the church, and as we met the children gave witness. Then we went down to the water. The schoolboys in a long stream went first, singing vigorously, the congregation straggled along anyhow, and we brought up the rear. The water lay like a mirror, reflecting the beautiful mountain. A soft light fell on it, half gold, half blue, and it looked like a lovely living thing, waiting to welcome the children. Then one by one they went in, breaking the gold and the blue into long bright ripples, and as each received her name – the name chosen and used before in expectation of this day – we on the bank sang, as is our custom, 'Jesus is our Life! Our life is Jesus!'"

Perhaps there would now be a quiet time for Amy, a time to find some tranquillity and renew her strength? She was so exhausted, she was in fact close to breakdown. She was ordered home but refused to go; instead she went earlier than usual to Ootacammund, known as 'The Queen of Hill Stations.' She took a dozen children with her, and looked forward to a time of refreshment and spiritual renewal in the cool climate, the peaceful green hills, forest, and grassland. She was particularly looking forward to her yearly stay at the home of her friend, Mrs. Hopwood. Sadly, however, there was to be no respite of spirit, but, rather, more trouble. News came to her that dysentery had broken out at Neyyoor. Her immediate reaction was to go there immediately, but a strongly worded wire was sent to her from Thomas Walker, advising her to stay where she was. Ponnammal, in charge of the children at Neyyoor, sent her a note urging her to remain, and to be like Moses: pray while the people were fighting on the plain. Ten children died in the epidemic. Amy's tribute to Ponnammal's leadership in the crisis is unstinting: "As for our dear Ponnammal, her faith rose until I could only use the word 'heroic' when I think of her. Weak and frail herself, she kept all going quietly and in an orderly fashion. She inspired her nurses with her own beautiful courage. One – the only unconverted nurse we had – was converted. Nothing had ever touched her before." '. . . so it has been life out of death,' wrote Ponnammal."

Soon the breathtaking views from Ootacammund in the Western Ghat Mountains were left behind once more. Amy returned to the cauldron of troubles that lay ahead, as from Dohnavur she continued to challenge the giant of child abuse of South India. She summed up her attitude to the recent disease crisis in some brave words:

"By the time the fire had leave to touch us, its power to injure had been taken from it; it had only power to refine." She further comments, "We have often prayed that this work should be through and through pure: 'We would be melted in the heat of love, by flames far fiercer than are blown to prove, and purge the silver ore adulterate.' If this is God's answer to our prayers, we would not shrink from it. With our wills, we say, 'Work on'. Our feelings would say, 'Stay Thy hand'; but oh to live in the realm of our will, not in the realm of our feelings. And may our wills be energised 'til truly and honestly we do not want our own at all, but only absolutely His."

Amy could plainly see that the need for more medical help at Dohnavur was paramount, either Indian or otherwise. The strain of leading the work was immense, and the loneliness of leadership was real. Her heart cry – for that is exactly what it was – emerges in her writing. In her second *Scrap* letter of 1907, she wonders if her desire for more medical help at Dohnavur is too great a gift to ask.

"Sometimes I wonder if God will ever give me a comrade, who will be such a comrade: utterly other-worldly, utterly single-hearted, utterly consumed. Don't think I mean that I am myself! I fall far short of my own standards. But this is what I want to be, and that is what we must be if we are to stand the strain and conquer. A heart-friend of His choice, maybe Indian, who before coming would have learned to know God in such wise that all that usually attracts would have lost power over her. But if this is not His thought, then pray that some other help may be sent, or that I may be given double strength. Anything rather than the wrong one."

Despite the trials she faced, her faith overcame her fears, and Christian hope conquered hopelessness. "This battle is the Lord's," she tells her prayer warriors. "All over South India, so many are perishing. Oh, to reach and save far more." The woman who delighted in the Lord was to be given the desires of her heart.

Starry, Starry Night

12 IT WAS 1912. On January 17th Captain Robert Scott and his valorous companions, Wilson, Bowes, Evans, and Oates, reached the South Pole, only to discover that they had been beaten to it one month before by their Norwegian rivals, led by the great Explorer, Roald Amundsen. All five Britons perished on their return journey; the last three survivors were trapped in their tent by a blizzard with almost no fuel or food, and died just eleven miles from a food depot.

Another tragedy dominated World News in 1912; and it still haunts mankind's collective memory. On her maiden voyage from Southampton to New York, the most famous ship since Noah's Ark (and built in Belfast), the *Titanic*, struck an iceberg. The unthinkable happened. She was reckoned to be unsinkable, but on the morning of April 15th more than 1,500 of the 2,340 passengers and crew drowned in the icy waters of the North Atlantic. Fred Fleet, one of the lookouts, said he could have saved the ship if he had had a pair of binoculars. His request for binoculars was ignored, and the great ship was lost for want of a pair of glasses.

On August 20th General William Booth died at 83 years of age. Booth had been expelled from two Methodist Churches, because he wanted to preach in the open air. He got his wish, and the world got the Salvation Army. In India, on December 23rd a bomb was hurled at the Governor General of India, Lord Hardinge, as he rode on the back of an elephant into Delhi. He was taking part in a Durbar to celebrate the handing over of India's new capital. He and his wife survived, but he was seriously wounded. Sadly, an attendant was killed. At the same Durbar, Lady Lawley privately told Queen Mary some of the facts which she had requested Amy Carmichael to compile. The Queen sent Amy a message of sympathy.

1912 found Amy as busy as ever. The intervening years had seen changes at Dohnavur. In 1907, Mabel Wade arrived. She was the first European to join Amy on a permanent basis. Mabel was a trained nurse from Yorkshire. She had huge responsibilities, as there was no doctor on the team, but she responded magnificently. In those early days, Amy's work attracted a lot of criticism. She wrote of 'The Calm Community of the Criticised'. Quite a movement arose among missionaries and Indian Christians, to 'get Amy Carmichael out of India'. Her implacable opposition to mere nominal Christianity, the high standard of Godliness expected in her fellow workers, her wearing of the sari, and her dependence on faith and prayer for funds, drew deep opposition. She was accused of being a dictator, of being opposed to marriage; and that her attempt to save Temple children was only a stunt to draw attention to herself. She weathered it all, maintaining that, as she wrote years later, "it is not at all that we think that ours is the only way of living, but we are sure that it is the way meant for us."

There were encouragements as well as discouragements, of course. In July 1907 – "one glorious day," as Amy put it – a letter came to her, saying that the writer had it on her heart to do something in memory of her departed mother. The writer and a friend had united to send a gift of £200, paid into the Bank of Madras, to build new nurseries. It was the largest single gift she had ever received, and made it possible in March 1908 for Ponnammal and the babies from Neyyoor to join the Dohnavur family permanently.

In March 1909, a child called Muttammal arrived with her mother on Amy's verandah in Dohnavur. The mother begged for protection, and the story of Muttammal and her relationship with

Amy Carmichael began. It has been well documented by Amy, and clearly penned by Bishop Houghton and others. At one stage, the protection of Muttammal threatened to bring seven years of imprisonment for Amy, but it did not happen. It involved quite a few appearances in Court, where at one stage Amy admitted "the Irish in me surfaced." After many adventures for Muttammal, involving journeys from Ceylon to China, she eventually married Arul Dasan, who belonged to the Dohnavur family, and settled at Dohnavur. Amy had had a dream, in which she saw the marriage ceremony taking place, before anything had actually happened between them.

So the work progressed, as the Dohnavur family grew. Amy grew too, spiritually, and in leadership qualities as she became 'mother' to so many. Obviously, there were discipline problems in raising so many children; and she did not shrink from applying that discipline. She also did not shrink from sitting down with a growing child, to tell her what she had been saved from. Many came as babies, and had no idea what Temple life would unquestionably have entailed. Amy did this on what she called 'Coming Days'. When a child came to Dohnavur the date was recorded and celebrated every year as her 'Coming Day'. On that day, early in the morning she was allowed to have tea with Amy in her room, and receive some

scented soap, a card, and the opportunity to select something from Amy's intriguing gift cupboard. Then the talk would follow, on what her 'Coming' had prevented. Amy would also remind each girl of the meaning of the name she had been given when she arrived at Dohnavur. "Amma took hold of my hand," one recalled, "and said, 'I give you your name 'Star', that you might be a shining star for the Lord Jesus.'"

Amy loved to stargaze, and the awesomeness of the stars was not lost on her. Today, NASA scientists are using a £52m camera on the Hubble space telescope. It is unveiling the most spectacular views of the rest of the universe ever seen by human beings. The furthermost object observed is the Tadpole Galaxy, which is 430 million light years away! Obviously, Amy didn't have access to the Hubble space telescope, but writing in her *Scraps* of January 1912 she records that recently she got the children up at 5.30 a.m. to stargaze. She explains that the children had asked her where their special stars had gone: "the stars they saw last October and November at bed time, after which they had named their best beloved dolls." The teacher in Amy, whose love for the Shepherd of the Stars was undimmed, had been busy. After all, God calls all the stars by name, and *brings out their host by number* (see Isaiah 40:25-26). The little girls of Dohnavur obviously enjoyed taking the stars' names for their best-loved dolls. "So," writes Amy, "this morning as I got up it struck me that they would enjoy seeing Orion and his fellows, who had reappeared in the early morning sky."

The sheer enjoyment of that morning so long ago still bubbles in Amy's prose. It is clear that she enjoyed it every bit as much as the children did. "As they looked up," she relates, "they danced with excitement, when they saw their old friends. 'Oh, there's Orion.' 'Where?' 'There! Look at Rigal.' Then shouts of 'Betelgeuze' . . . they could hardly find the Pleiades and the Hyades, as there was a little moonlight; but Alder Barin shone out, and the great favourite, Capella, (much disappointment as her kids were invisible); and they could see Perseus' three bright stars, and Andromeda's. There was great excitement over these finds, as Tara's 'child' is Andromeda, and Evu's is Perseus. Then, as they turned to the South West, there was a shout of 'Canopus!' 'Achanar!' The greatest rapture, however, was naturally poured upon Sirius, whose flashing colours survive even in the moonlight."

As we saw earlier, Amy believed Samuel Rutherford's teaching that when a child dies it is not lost to the mother, because he or she is 'found to Christ'. Let me just repeat his wonderful statement, "Like unto a star which, going out of our sight, doth not die and vanish but shineth in another hemisphere, you see her not; yet she doth shine in another country." One of Amy's most deeply-loved children – if not, in fact, her most deeply loved child, a star of stars – was soon to slip out of her sight to shine in another country, and it just about broke Amy's heart. "I had hoped," Amy admitted, "to put only bright things in this letter, and now brightness seems far; for our darling little Lulla, leader of kindergarten games and all nursery joys, has left us. I can hardly believe it yet."

Lulla, a five year old Brahman child, took ill in August 1912. Amy's description of her approaching death is poignant:

"I cannot write, even to those who knew her, of the next few hours. The doctor did not come, and every moment added to the dreadful distress for breath. At about 8.30 I could bear it no longer – to see that patient child suffer so, was just too much – and I went to Ponnammal's room and besought the Lord to take her. When I came back a few minutes later Mabel startled me by saying, "She has been smiling." I could hardly believe it. I had asked for peace, not joy. In another moment, I saw it. Such a smile as I had ever seen, lit that lovely little face. She threw out her arms, smiling eagerly, and clasped her hands with all her strength. Ponnammal was at her feet, Mabel was holding the pillow under her head, I was beside her. We all three gazed in awe. None of us had ever seen such a thing before – that radiant, conscious, joyous smile on a dying child's face; and to see her clasp her hands – was it not wonderful? Then Lulla turned to Mabel, pulled down her face with her little hands in a caressing way that was always special to her and kissed it. Then she turned to me, panting for breath as she was, pulled my face down flinging her arms round my neck, and she tried to kiss me and stroked my face, but the dear little arms fell back.

God gave me strength at that moment to do what I had been longing to do: I sang the first verse of the *Good Night Hymn* to her. Never had it held so much meaning:

Jesus, tender Shepherd, hear me,
Bless Thy little lamb tonight.
Through the darkness be Thou near me,
Keep me safe till Morning Light.

A few minutes later, and the night had passed for Lulla. Our little treasure was in Morning Light."

Amy Carmichael did not apologise for sharing the reality of the work in which she was so deeply and emotionally involved. "I did not mean to send a sad letter out after so many months of silence, but if you share the battle with us you must share the battle wounds." She then adds a postscript of a wound that must have penetrated her life more deeply than words could capture.

Postscript. September 8th 1912:

"I must compel myself to write what, even as I write it, I can hardly yet believe: our leader and strong tower of courage and comfort – father and brother to us all, has been suddenly taken from us. He was holding a mission in the Telugu country. Cholera came to him. It was God's swift messenger – he was crowned upon the battlefield.

. . . as little Lulla entered in, we saw something of the joy which had been given, even to a child – what must that joy be to the saint and warrior, when all the trumpets sound 'for him' on the other side?

. . . it may be that the inner story of the letter may have its word for someone. For us, it is now absolutely overshadowed by the far more tremendous parting which so soon followed it. And, yet, we cannot forget that one little, bright glimpse was given us 'into the Joy of the Lord.'

Yours, in the certainty of the Blessed Hope,

Amy Wilson-Carmichael."

The death of *The Iyer*, Thomas Walker, removed the light of one of the most illustrious stars in Amy's firmament. The Bible tells us that the godly Daniel was once addressed by the man clothed in linen, one sent by God: *'those who are wise will shine like the brightness of the heavens; and those who lead many to righteousness, like the stars forever and* ever' (Daniel 12:3). For Amy Carmichael, 1912 was certainly a year of stars moving on to shine elsewhere. She must have wondered what on earth was coming next. Yet her faith was firm. In her poem, *God of the stars*, she wrote:

> I am the God of the stars.
> They do not lose their way;
> Not one do I mislay.
> Their times are in My Hand;
> They move at My command.
>
> I am the God of the stars.
> Today, as yesterday,
> The God of thee and thine,
> Less thine they are than Mine;
> And shall Mine go astray?
>
> I am the God of the stars.
> Lift up thine eyes and see,
> As far as mortal may,
> Into Eternity;
> And stay thy heart on Me.

The Moon In My Cup Of Tea

13

IT WAS 1915. Albert Einstein postulated a new theory of gravity, and Robert Frost's *North of Boston* was published in the United States. W. G. Grace, who had scored 54,896 runs and taken 2,876 wickets in his lifetime, died. Henry Ford produced his one-millionth car, and Ivor Novello wrote the war song, *Keep the Home Fires Burning*.

The First World War raged furiously in all sorts of corners. In January, a German Zeppelin crossed the Norfolk coast and bombed Great Yarmouth and King's Lynn. In February, the Royal Navy carried war to the Turkish enemy, and battle cruisers opened up a bombardment of the forts guarding the Dardanelles. Germany set a submarine blockade of the British Isles, with the threat that any vessels moving in UK waters would be seen as 'fair game'. In May, the huge Cunard liner *Lusitania* sank off the Irish coast, torpedoed without warning by a German submarine. The ship was only eight miles off the Old Head of Kinsale. In August, the great Russian fortress of Brest-Litovsk fell to the Germans. On October 12th, Edith Cavell, the gifted and dedicated nurse, was executed in Brussels.

By November 1915, the Italian death-toll in the war was 250,000; and by December, as the allies retreated from the ill-fated Gallipoli expedition, the House of Commons had been told that the

Dardanelles casualties were 25,000 dead, 76,000 wounded, 13,000 missing, and 96,000 sick admitted to hospital.

In India, Amy Carmichael continued at Dohnavur, with what she called 'the War of the Lord'. Death was never far away in all she faced; in 1915 it took another of her dearest friends and colleagues. It is of value to reflect on Amy's attitude to the death of her colleagues, for there is much to learn from it. In October 1912, for example, her *Dohnavur Letter*, as *Scraps* was now called, carried two poems that epitomise her feelings at the death of her mentor, counsellor and teacher, Thomas Walker:

> There is no 'getting over' sorrow,
> But there is a 'getting into' sorrow;
> And finding right in the heart of it
> The dearest of all human beings –
> The Man of Sorrows.

> A voice is heard on earth of kinsfolk weeping
> The loss of one they love;
> But he is gone where the redeemed are keeping
> A festival above.
> The mourners throng the way,
> And, from the steeple,
> The funeral bell tolls slow;
> But, on the Golden Street, the holy people
> Are passing to and fro,
> And saying as they meet, 'Rejoice! Another,
> Long waited for, is come!
> The Saviour's heart is glad: Another brother
> Hath reached the Father's home.

The loss she felt is palpable in the letter. It is, as ever, full of spirituality; and yet it still highlights, in poignant detail, life in all its swirling circumstances. She describes their last morning together:

"Next morning as usual we had tea at 6.00 a.m., in moonlight as our clocks were a little fast. He had laughed at me the morning before, saying I had the moon reflected in my cup of tea. It was a little less bright that Monday morning, August 12th, but still it was the soft light between moonshine and dawn; and by 6.20a.m. it was only just light enough to see to read Psalms for the Day. He read them to us as usual, and we stopped over the wonderful

word in the 63rd: *Thus have I looked for thee in holiness that I might behold thy power and glory.* It was the last verse we looked over together.

Fifteen minutes later he was off for Masulipatam. It was clear dawn then, and I shall never forget that bright, short, Goodbye, as he set off for his last campaign. "God be with you. Goodbye." He was off; and, as usual, before he had reached the gate he was deep in his book. It was the sort of Goodbye he would have chosen.

As the bandy turned down the lane, our faithful old Sundarie came out to say 'Salam'. "Salam, Sundarie!" he called out to her, "I go and come." 'Go and come' is the idiom of the country, but now it holds so much; he has gone and he will come: what a coming it will be!"

The Scripture, *What I do thou knowest not now, but thou shalt know hereafter*, was the text which Amy called 'the most loving word', after the loss of Thomas Walker. Yet she also made this challenging statement, even in the light of the message of the Scripture text that brought her the most comfort: "I sometimes feel it will be just as perfect whether or not it is explained, because we know our Father; so we know His secrets cannot possibly contain anything but love." From the depths of Amy's sorrow, however, she reacted strongly to some of the letters of sympathy she received. To all who may have to write them, her reactions give a word of consummate warning for any generation:

"Sometimes letters come which, however kind in purpose, do not strike me as at all true in view. 'It is very hard to see how this can be for the best' – but we are not asked to see, and why need we then to know? . . . 'It is such an irreparable loss, that it is very hard to trust all for the best' – truly it is an irreparable loss, but is it faith at all if it is 'hard to trust' when things are entirely bewildering? There is something in this kind of talk, which makes me feel like sympathising with the Father who hears it. I feel as if He must feel a little as I should, if I heard Tara and Evu discussing something I had done, and finishing up with 'It is very hard to trust Amma'. For really, isn't that what such talk comes to? Oh, let us have done with it!"

Amy's true comfort was to be found in the fact that God is the hand behind history, including our own personal history. Her view is perfectly stated in her exposition of Psalm 47:4 - *He chose our inheritance for us, the pride of Jacob whom he loved*. "The word *chose* is the same word as that used in 1 Samuel 17:40. Isn't it a vivid picture? David did not pick up five stones haphazardly. He chose, after testing (Heb.), the five best suited for his purpose, and our Father does not choose our set of circumstances less carefully . . . It is easy to write it. May God save us from 'paper grace', and give us grace to live it, and to continue to live it!"

There were some significant changes in 1913. The family at Dohnavur had risen to around one hundred and forty in number. To Amy's great relief, two sisters, Edith and Agnes Naish, who for many years had been involved in missionary work at Palmcottah, came to help her after Thomas Walker's death. They joined the Fellowship the following year. Agnes Naish, a teacher, was put in charge of the children's education. Arul Dasan took on the vital role of superintending the building work. In August that year, thirty-three children were baptised.

Continuing trouble was never very far away. Ponnammal took seriously ill with cancer, and Amy nursed her through two operations. Then malaria struck, and seventy of the children were ill at the same time. In July 1913, Mrs. Carmichael died in London. Was there any relief for Amy, as sorrow after sorrow, trial after trial, stress almost beyond human endurance, came in waves upon her life? The truth is that, in the midst of it all, the creativity flowing from Amy's life heightened. Many of the songs sung by the

Dohnavur family were, as Amy would have put it, 'taken' during this time. The Lord gave them, Amy took them and wrote them down. Two were written on the brown paper of a medicine bottle as she travelled! Her friend over at the Salvation Army hospital at Neyyoor, Dr. Turner, wrote the music for her songs. This heightened creativity began as Amy nursed Ponnammal at night in hospital at Nagercoil. No hour was wasted, and Amy's redeeming of time was awesome.

As if all these trials were not enough, another arose in December 1913, when the threat of a prison sentence faced her. A five-year-old Temple child called Kohila had been settled at Dohnavur for a year, when her guardians wrote demanding that she be returned to them. If Amy refused to return the child, her guardians threatened that they would charge her with kidnapping. There are times when a Christian is governed by a higher law that clashes with an earthly law; and in Kohila's case, as in Muttammal's earlier, Amy felt this was one of those times. She knew very well what she would have been returning the child to, and plans were made to send her to missionaries hundreds of miles away for protection, pending the decision of the Court. Amy told her Indian women workers that in a week's time she might be in prison.

If things went against her, Amy was determined to own up to what she had done and take the consequences, which was seven years' imprisonment. She would not appeal any decision of the Court. She knew the cost, and was prepared to pay it to save the child. Her colleague, Ponnammal, was dying, but bravely she said "Do not think of me." The Indian women workers all pled for the privilege, if possible, of standing substitute for Amy and going to prison in her place! The very next day a telegram came to Dohnavur, saying, "Criminal case dismissed!" The relief from that telegram for Amy and her colleagues was never to be forgotten.

Just as the 1914-18 war was about to break in Europe, mercifully Amy had been guided to purchase more land: a large field, which was set aside for a market garden. One of the Indian workers, Arul Dasan, was given several months' training by the Department of Agriculture in the cultivation of vegetables. As the war progressed, the field proved to be very valuable indeed, as the value of money gifts to the work at Dohnavur plummeted because of adverse exchange rates. Their purchasing power fell, until £1 had shrunk to four shillings.

How did the work cope during the difficult war years? There was, of course, the terror of submarines, and mail being lost because of enemy action. As the war neared its end Amy commented, "When the war began I asked our Father so to arrange matters that not one mail should pass empty. I knew that the war would make a great difference in the resources of His people, but then He had foreseen it when He caused us to embark upon this big adventure. He caused a little cloud to float down out of the blue, and rain upon one single dry field on the plain, while all the fields about it lay glowing in sunshine. We who were up on the mountains above Dohnavur saw it. But, after all, we are only children grown up, and I did want something every mail; so I asked for it. Not a single mail has been empty since that day."

Perhaps the most overriding principle Amy followed through the war years is found in her comment, "It is to Him, and not to His people, we look." Yet she does not diminish in any way the kindness of those who supported her work. In 1919, after the war was over, Amy wrote:

"In the most wonderful way all through the war, money has been sent to us for the furtherance of this War. A brother goes to Paradise, and his sister sends a gift because he loved little children. A gunner comes through unscathed and he sends his gift, for his new experience has made his heart more tender than ever towards all suffering. A mother has suffered more than words can tell and found God's grace sufficient, and she thanks Him by easing some mother-heart here."

In my research into Amy's archives, I came across a rare photograph of Amy at a Madras Beach, sitting with some of her girls in a stranded boat, watching the tide. She had taken fourteen of them on a trip to the city, and they were obviously enjoying the experience. They went to a jeweller's and saw uncut stones, they visited factories and shops and museums, they saw motor cars for the first time, and there is a beautiful photograph of some of the girls sitting on a motorcycle and in a sidecar, obviously delighted. To their amazement, they were shown 'moving pictures'. Yet, for me, that photograph of Amy Carmichael speaks more than the proverbial 'a thousand words'. I held a magnifying glass close to its surface, and somehow there, etched on Amy Carmichael's face, are the marks of the strain and stress of her huge responsibilities. There is only one phrase I can think of, to describe what that look so silently and powerfully conveys – *a living sacrifice*. The marks of those years of challenging such horrendous evil, and caring for the endless needs of others, are plain to see. How, then, did Amy keep on keeping on? Her poem, *Too great for Thee*, based on Elijah's experience when he told the Lord that he'd had enough (see 1 Kings 19:5-8), shows the secret of Amy's continuance, in the face of seemingly overwhelming odds.

An angel touched me, and he said to me,
 "The journey, pilgrim, is too great for thee.
But rise and eat and drink;
Thy food is here,
Thy Bread of Life,
Thy cruse of Water clear,
Drawn from the brook that doth as yesterday
Flow by the way.

And thou shalt go in strength of that pure food,
Made thine by virtue of the sacred Rood,
Unto the Mount of God;
Where thy Lord's face
Shall shine on thee,
On thee in thy low place,
Down at His feet who was thy Strength and Stay
Through all the Way."

O, Cake of Bread, baken on coals of fire –
Sharp fires of pain;

O, Water, turned to Wine –
Thy word is true; this food is daily mine.
Then never, never can the journey be
Too great for me.

Seven months after Thomas Walker died, Amy Carmichael experienced one of the greatest losses in her life. On August 26th 1915, after two years and five months of suffering, Ponnammal died. For eight years with *The Starry Cluster*, Ponnammal had been Amy's companion and colleague. In all the years that followed, she had been a loyal and faithful friend in the work of saving and caring for Temple children. She was often in a torment of pain, in the last stages of her cancer. "For the last month," Amy wrote, "she has been walking through the valley of the shadow of death. I never knew how dense that shadow could become, for I never before watched by anyone dying in this slow terrible way." She adds, "Yesterday, for example, she could only say one wistful little sentence: 'I had hoped to be able to stay with you and help you to bear the burden – but it is not to be.'" The One who bore her burdens as no other, called her to shine for Him in another place. As Amy put it, she did not believe in praying "Thy will be changed," but "Thy will be done." It was a heart-breaking parting, as the Dohnavur family filled Ponnammal's room with beautiful flowers, and surrounded her with great sprays of white jasmine. The children came in groups, and the village people too. A hundred children and girls eventually followed her cortège into the village street. Despite its sadness, as they sang together the children sought to show in the funeral service the 'triumphant hope of glory', and the village people crowded around to witness a sight they had never seen before. For Amy, it was a time of seeing so much stripped away. Her innermost feelings are, surely, caught in her poem *Strange Ashes*:

But these strange ashes, Lord? this nothingness,
This baffling sense of loss?
"Son, was the anguish of My stripping less
Upon the torturing Cross?

Was I not brought into the dust of death,
A worm, and no man, I?
Yea, turned to ashes by the vehement breath
Of fire – on Calvary?

O son beloved, this is thy heart's desire:
This, and no other thing
Follows the fall of the Consuming Fire
On the burnt offering.

Go now and taste the joy set high, afar –
No joy like that for thee –
See how it lights thy way, like some great star.
Come now and follow Me."

In December 1915, it looked as though Amy was going to have to bear the death of another of her dearest colleagues. Arulai had first heard the gospel when she was ten years old at an open air service in her village. Known as 'Star of Grace', she had become a real pillar of the work at Dohnavur. Suffering from nephritis, she came close to death.

"One day," wrote Amy, "it was one of the worst days – I faced for the first time a possible parting with this treasure of all treasures. It was not only her own preciousness, which made it a tremendous thing to part; it was her own preciousness to the whole work. *The Iyer*, Ponnammal, Arulai – our three strongest spiritual influences, the three upon whom I could always count for strength of character as well as for spiritual power – 'Lord, must Thou take them all?' was the question of my heart." As it turned out, Arulai was spared and lived for another 24 years, ever a 'Star of Grace'.

What was Amy's summary of those momentously sad times? It is worth pondering deeply her words at the end of her *Dohnavur Letter* of January 1916:

"All we have needed has come through these months, and the year has been richer, perhaps, than any other in spiritual victories. Children have been saved in most wonderful ways; and our dear girls have gone on this last year into fresh lands of promise – for, thank God, the War of the Lord has gone on; and we have not dared to follow the advice given in, I rejoice to say, very few letters, 'to curtail – as it sometimes is God's will to curtail even good work.' To curtail? With us it means to send children back to the temples: which child shall we send first?"

1916 saw the publication of Amy's biography of Thomas Walker, *Walker of Tirunelveli*. In her Introduction, she gives her view of him: "In India, we do not paint our teak; we let it show its grain. Poorer stuff is painted, teak asks for no pretence; and this book deals with teak." She quotes a Tirunelveli missionary, who, between College classes early in 1913, wrote of his view of Thomas Walker. He quotes lines from John Oxenham, which summarise his own view of Amy's mentor:

> 'Greatheart is dead,' they say:
> But the light shall burn the brighter,
> And the night shall be the lighter
> For his going;
> And a rich, rich harvest for his sowing.

As the Great War surged on to its final throes, with all that war entails, Amy Carmichael was proving that the struggle against *principalities and powers, and spiritual wickedness in high places* was just as real, and just as costly. May her thoughts on the loss of her colleagues, and the ultimate victory assured by the Captain of her salvation, have resonance for us all.

———•——— The Laughing Place

14 IT WAS 1917. On April 2nd President Woodrow
Wilson called to a joint session of Congress for the
———•——— United States to go to war, saying, "The world must
be made safe for democracy." Cheers in the public galleries greeted
him; but on his return to the White House it was reported that he
said, "My message was one of death for young men. How odd it
seems to applaud that." He then put his head in his hands and
wept.

By the time the First World War had spent itself, Germany had
lost over a million men, as had Austria and Hungary. Russia lost
around two million, and Britain three quarters of a million, plus
two hundred thousand from its Empire, of whom nearly one-third
were Indians. Actually, as a proportion of the total manpower of all
British garrisons in the Empire, the Indian Army accounted for well
over 62%. France had a death toll almost twice as high as Britain's.
Italy lost around half a million men, and Turkey the same. As the
poet Wilfred Owen, who was killed in the war, had so powerfully
highlighted, anyone who witnessed the carnage of the war would
not with zest tell the old lie, 'Dulce et decorum est pro patria mori' –
'it is sweet and fitting to die for one's country.'

In 1917, Tsar Nicholas II signed the form of abdication in the
Imperial Train, and was exiled with his family to Western Siberia

where eventually they were all mercilessly shot. Communism was beginning to grip Russia, and its 'Iron Curtain' was beginning to descend.

As the New Year began, however, freedom came for one little boy at Dohnavur. On January 14th 1918, he arrived at the Dohnavur bungalow in the arms of a very tired Arul. They arrived in a bandy, to be greeted with enthusiasm. The little child held its thin little arms out to Amy, and soon the weary little head was resting contentedly on her shoulders. Amy remembered thinking, "I wish you were a boy." Her wish was granted; for, five minutes after he had been carried off to the nursery, a racing, breathless Mabel Wade returned with the news, "It's a boy!" That late evening was a very significant time in the history of the Dohnavur family and in Amy's ministry. As we shall see, she had prayed for ten years that a work for boys might be established. It was in September 1917 that God gave her confirmation about it in the Grey Jungle. The Grey Jungle? – therein lies a tale.

It was Brer Rabbit, the famous, fictitious rabbit in the memorable children's stories by that gentle newspaperman, Joel Chandler Harris, who spoke of everyone needing a 'Laughing Place.' For Amy

and her charges, was there such a place? Taking children to Ootacamund in the hot season had become a costly affair; and, with such a large family, absence from Dohnavur at such a distance was not practical. Amy decided to take the children for a year or two to a Government Forest Department bungalow in the mountains above Dohnavur, at a place called Sengelteri. It was cool in the mountains, and the children loved to play in the river and at the waterfall. It was not only the children who loved to play – the Wild-bird child was also in her element. Amy explained 'the expedition' to Sengelteri:

"It was rather an experiment: I wanted to find out if the place would be good for the workers and children, who must sometimes get out of the compound if they are not to fossilise. Such a place needed to be near, as the expenses of carting a big family about is considerable. It had to be near for me, too, as at present it is impossible to be long out of the reach of Dohnavur, in case of need. Sengelteri is only five or six hours distant by quick coolie runner."

That Amy needed to get out of the compound in order not to fossilise is also clear, when one reads the tale of Amy and the growling bear! At Sengelteri, in an area full of the tracks of tiger, elephant and deer, one day Amy was returning with three children from a walk in the forest to the bungalow, when she saw the other children coming back from the river. They had found some bear holes on their walk, and so, just for the fun of it, Amy and the three children hid behind the trees and growled, pretending to be bears. The other children rushed wildly up to the bungalow, and then, to Amy's immense gratification that they cared enough about her, the whole household turned out with sticks, the children making a dive for the wood, where they thought their Amma was being devoured! When Amy and the others emerged calmly, and asked what the matter was, they hollered, "Bears! Bears! Hasten!" When one of the leaders was about to raise a prayer of thanks for their deliverance, a little girl giggled, and the game was well and truly up!

Amy had seen the advantages of a trip away to the mountains, but Sengelteri could not accommodate all who needed to go; and even if it had, the property belonged to the Government for its own use. "I had for years felt," Amy commented, "there might be a place high enough to be convenient; but no one seemed to feel it a possible plan at all." That no one else felt it to be feasible was no deterrent to her. Having proved the worth of Sengelteri, she felt compelled to try to do something. "I set to work, to explore," she wrote. Her exploration was to lead to a lot of happiness, and God knew that she needed some. "There is nothing so stimulating as happiness," she wrote on October 31st 1917; "yesterday brought us a new happiness and it acts today like a big wave, carrying me over various hindering things that lie between you and a letter. That is why you are having one so soon again . . . now for the story of it."

She tells of a workman who knew every inch of the mountain, who said, "Up there . . . is the very place for you," indicating a recess under some glorious crags that lay at the back of Dohnavur. Amy set off with a party to have a look, "feeling like a fly being strongly cooked, as it crawled up an oven door." (Ah, there speaks the poet in her!) But it was not the place for her or her children for quite a number of reasons, including a nearby land slip! So, the search continued. Then she was told enthusiastically of another place called, because of its beauty, 'Vishnu's Heaven'. Amy started at 3.30 a.m., and was half way up the foothills by dawn. Again, the site proved to be unsuitable.

The search for a 'Laughing Place' continued. One evening, Amy found herself 4,000 feet up in the mountains sleeping on the mud floor of a disused coffee plantation. It was so cold that two of the older girls kept a fire burning all night. On the way down, they met a kind Brahmin who knew the forest well. Learning of their quest, he casually mentioned a place he knew, called 'The Grey Jungle'. The steps of this good woman were being ordered by the Lord: the Brahmin's suggestion was no casual remark, for it led to Amy Carmichael's 'Laughing Place', and to probably the nearest place to Heaven that Amy was to know on earth.

"The whole side of the gorge had always looked so grey in comparison to the lovely green of our particular gorge, that I had not been attracted to it," she wrote, "and no one had ever suggested it as the very least possible. Well, we went – F.B., a troop of children, and I, and the moment we saw it we knew we had found our hearts' desire. How could I describe it? It sets you singing, however dull you are. First comes the walk up to it. Oh, how you want everyone you love to share it. Some, however, would find its front door prohibitive. It is a little straight cliff, up which you climb as best you can. It will have to be made safer, as a slip there would mean a funeral.

The ravine down which you finally scramble is wide and deep. There are huge forest trees, with curly monkey swings, as we call them, overhead; but it was the water which drew us – a waterfall – a bathing pool. Water, and no leeches.

. . . the children were wild with joy over an orange tree covered with fruit, and not realising it was in a body's property they wanted to fall upon it at once. Guavas, a fruit they love, grew there too, and small pineapples. The thought came, 'Oh, to have this place'; but it hardly shaped itself into a wish."

It was a truly beautiful place. Green forest billowed up the mountains as far as the eye could see, with rocky mountain tops peaking out to cap the scene. A pool deep enough for diving, having a floor of clean, white sand, was such a pool that Amy said, "it washed troubles off, and just kissed worries away." The rock pools of her childhood in Millisle were still in Amy's subconscious; and though Ireland's 'forty shades of green' were something she would never see again in her lifetime, they were replaced in that Indian jungle. The scene is captured well in her poem, *The Cool Green Mere*:

I see a little cool, green mere,
Like to a ruffled looking-glass;
Where lovely green lights interfere
Each with the other, and then pass
In rippled patterns to the grey
Of rocks that bar their further way.

I hear a mingled music now:
A streamlet that has much to tell,
And two sweet birds that on a bough
Nearby love one another well.
And like a flake of summer sky,
A pale blue butterfly floats by.

A sudden sun-flash, and below,
Upon a rock of amber brown,
Bright golden sparkles come and go,
As if in their dim water-town,
Set on that lighted pedestal,
The water things held carnival.

The mountain wind blows in my face;
I see the water, smell the rain;
Yet I am here in mine own place,
With duties thronging me again –
But the more welcome, the more dear,
Because of you, my cool, green mere.

Prayer followed of course, and much discussion; but eventually it was decided to purchase the upper hillside, including "a splendid open grassy place backed by mountains, just the place for a forest house."

The owner, an older Mohammedan gentleman, asked for £100 for the 37 acres of hillside with the river running through it, constantly replenished at its source, including waterfalls, bathing pools (including *the* pool), huge trees, and green, luxuriant forest. There was a view across the plain to the Eastern Sea coast. Amy, as usual, asked for a sign from God, as to whether this 'kissing-your-worries-away' place for the rescued children and those who helped them was on! The very next day she opened her mail, to discover a letter from a lawyer in Cork, Ireland. The letter informed her that a friend of hers, whom she calls Florence P-, had left her £100 in a legacy. Thus, Amy had her 'sign'. Another letter from a friend followed, saying, "he wanted to give us the Grey Jungle. If I would tell him how much it cost, he would remit it." Amy wryly comments, "It did not cross my mind to hope for a raven in that envelope." Yet an 'Elijah's raven', there certainly was!

On September 14th 1917, the Grey Jungle was purchased. As Amy had said, it was a 'new happiness', and was to prove its worth to be beyond gold. Eventually, after many ups and downs – not least from caste-divided workers, rain, and building incompetence – a house called 'Forest House' was constructed.

At the Grey Jungle Amy loved to eat outdoors: to 'have tea' in the rarest places, including the tops of rocks. The children learned to swim in 'The Emerald Pool'. One day, tragedy nearly struck. A child who Amy was helping in the pool dragged her under, and she very nearly drowned. She brushed off the experience, but it was a serious one nonetheless.

For decades the Grey Jungle served as a cool place of solace and inspiration, not only from the searing heat of India's hot seasons, but as a place of quiet and aesthetic beauty for those who day and night served those in deep need. No one deserved such a place more than Amy Carmichael. It was here that she wrote many songs which the children learned by heart. All kinds of subjects, from elephants to the moon, were covered; and there can be no doubt that the mountain-land of the Grey Jungle was the nemesis for her creativity, calling up even this definitive line in one of her poems: "Be all my thoughts like wild bird's song, on this Thy day."

In September 1917, Amy went up to the Grey Jungle, heavily burdened about beginning a work for boys. She was standing in the rain, watching the waters rush over rocks in the river. As the endless flow of water rushed past, she thought of the huge need for adequate funds for such a project. It was wartime in the world: how would she cope with boys to care for, as well as girls? As she stood there, God spoke to her through the fact that 'the water flowed on'. The burden lifted! As recounted earlier in this chapter, January 14th 1918 saw the arrival of a tired little boy at Dohnavur. This was the beginning of Dohnavur's service to boys who were in need of help. Throughout her lifetime, the Wild-bird child from Ulster would often fly to the Grey Jungle, but never to roost. Other demands were always calling, and these demands, together with her response to them, are caught in her beautiful poem *Rise and Fly*. Few have risen for God with more determination, nor flown further in His service.

> House of the greenwood,
> Patterned the carpet
> Thy weaver weaves;
> Grey are thy walls,
> Fitly carved thy staircase,
> Purple thine eaves;
> High is thy house roof,
> Fashioned for beauty,

Very far spread;
Mighty thy lamps,
And thy candles forever
Bright overhead.

Various thy music:
Over thy harp strings
Great fingers sweep;
Light lilt of lullaby
Floats where the wind rocks
Treetops to sleep;
Hark to the lovable
White waters singing
Carols and glees;
Hark to the bird whistle,
Whispers of grasses,
Hum of the bees.

House of the greenwood,
Cleansing and healing
Thine influence;
Pure are thine airs,
Every room in thee holy
With Innocence.
And all throughout thee
Thy manifold voices
Speak the word plain:
  "Grovel not, rise ye;
Be bird-like, be dove-like;
Rise, fly again.
Down among pots
Though ye lay, yet aspire ye.
Was it not told,
God has prepared for you
Wings as of silver,
Feathers of gold?"

15 Looking At Jupiter, And Into A Chasm

IT WAS 1919. A scientist called Ernest Rutherford 'split' the atom, proving that atoms are not the indivisible particles they were once thought to be. President Wilson presided over the first meeting of The League of Nations in Paris, and, as Russia was gripped in a Civil War, Lenin sought to spark revolution throughout Europe.

At Scapa Flow in the Orkneys, German sailors, in a final act of defiance, opened the seacocks on seventy ships that had been interned, and scuttled them. On June 28th the Germans reluctantly signed the Versailles Peace Treaty.

In West Africa and Brazil, expeditions organised by the Royal Astronomical Society confirmed the revolutionary ideas embodied in Albert Einstein's *Theory of Relativity*. They found that the path of light from a star passing close to the sun was bent by its gravitational field, in exactly the way Einstein had predicted.

On November 28th 1919, Viscountess (Nancy) Astor, who was born in America, became Britain's first woman Member of Parliament to sit in the House of Commons. She announced her intention to dress plainly, saying, "I want to make it possible for the humblest woman who may be elected to follow the precedent I set."

On the question of humility, an interesting and totally unexpected circumstance had arisen in Amy Carmichael's life. In January 1919 she received a telegram from the Governor of Madras, Lord Pentland, congratulating her on being included in the Royal Birthday Honours List. She had been awarded the Kaiser-i-Hind Medal for her services to the people of India. Amy was shocked at the news. She wrote to Lord Pentland, asking if it would be unpardonably rude to ask to be allowed not to have it. She protested that she had done nothing to 'make it fitting', and told him that she was troubled to have an experience so different from "His, who was despised and rejected, not kindly honoured." It would have been fascinating to hear the conversation that ensued, as Amy's friends pressed upon her that it would be very ungracious to refuse such an honour. She relented, but refused to attend the presentation ceremony.

In the context of Amy's attitude to awards and distinctions, two of her poems eloquently give her inmost feelings about the matter. The first, entitled *Medals and Titles?*, warns against coveting them:

Medals and lighted titles? Who but is ashamed
That such, for such as we, should ever be claimed
As our just due? Perish the paltry plea,
The sordid thought. Oh, little, little have we
Done for our kind; that little, how faultily.
And, yet, what joy to do it! Has the day
When 'The Offscouring of All things' could be
An apostle's title wholly passed away?

Ah, but if one among us covets famed
Great orders – recognitions – let him lay
Close to his heart two ancient words, and say
Them over and over till he be
Somewhat attuned to them: Gethsemane
The first; the second, Calvary.

The second poem is probably Amy Carmichael's most famous. It is entitled *No Scar?*

Hast thou no scar?
No hidden scar on foot, or side, or hand?
I hear thee sung as mighty in the land;
I hear them hail thy bright, ascendant star.
Hast thou no scar?

Hast thou no wound?
Yet I was wounded by the archers: spent,
Leaned Me against a tree to die; and rent
By ravening beasts that compassed Me, I swooned.
Hast thou no wound?

No wound? No scar?
Yet, as the Master shall the servant be,
And pierced are the feet that follow Me.
But thine are whole; can he have followed far
Who has nor wound nor scar?

What kind of standard, then, did Amy expect in the kind of worker she desired for Dohnavur? In June 1919, she wrote in a letter: "Shall I say anything about the kind of worker we asked? She must be one who has been called to Dohnavur. The burning shame of this traffic in young children must have penetrated her inmost soul. Without that experience, that call, she will never stand up against all that joining us must mean. She must be a missionary, and she must be qualified." Amy did not take Government aid for her work, because she felt the children would have to face too much exam pressure, and "not have enough time left over for other things." Wisely she adds, "We want our children to grow up with the thought of service for their God and their country . . . Just because we are not 'government', we must be careful to do as much for our children as if we were; and perhaps more."

Even in delineating the qualities she looked for in a worker for Dohnavur, Amy does not leave out a metaphor from the natural world: "She must be patient. Sometimes on a moonlight night when

the sky is clear electric blue, I have seen Jupiter poised alone in that wonderful transparent depth of height, and wondered at the quiet glory of it. Not even the brilliant moonlight overwhelms the great glory of it. But it looks far, far overhead; further away than when as on either nights a thousand stars shine round about it. I think our ideal is something like that in its far awayness, its strange solitariness and its calm glory too. We need to be very patient, for our hope is very high."

Amy tells of a leaflet that arrived at Dohnavur, highlighting the extraordinary devotion of Evangelists and others in India and elsewhere. She comments:

"The type of worker described in that leaflet is not typical. I could not help wondering, as I read it aloud at the breakfast table, what the Christian public, which is fed on such descriptions, would feel if it too could have sat at breakfast with us as I read those fascinating sentences. 'Are you making it up? It sounds like a fairytale,' was one interrupting remark; and our newest recruit added, 'It's what everyone at home is told. They all believe it; they hear nothing else.'

As I read, I thought of the many letters I had received from men and women missionaries during the last twenty years or more, letters always destroyed as soon as read and answered. 'Disillusioned' was the under-word of all those letters. So, there must be something of the pioneer about the one we need. The fields are all untrodden where she will have to walk. She must have seen visions and she must have dreamt dreams, and yet she must be humble and loving enough to plod along in patience that will not get tired."

There is no doubt that the burning shame of the traffic in young children had penetrated Amy Carmichael's innermost soul. A letter in January 1917 tells of the purchase of the land at the Grey Jungle. The purchase showed great foresight, but it did not diminish Amy's near-sighted focus on her immediate priority. The letter tells of a visit to a Festival connected with the opening of a door in the temple, kept closed all year round except during the ten days following the fourth day of January. Amy and her five colleagues arrived in the town in the late afternoon, and Amy took them through a side door in the temple wall and walked about in the temple courts. "They saw," she writes, "a little way into India. We had books to give to the people there and gave them quietly." She points out that it was helpful to be wearing the native dress.

There then follows such writing that holds descriptive powers equal to Rudyard Kipling and E. M. Forster. It is included here as a tribute to a woman who laid her hugely gifted pen at the sorely wounded feet of Christ, the Light of the World:

"These temple courts and corridors are impressive even in daylight, when the dust of ages is visible, and the huge grotesque stone carvings stare openly at you, as you, a mere ant in comparison, walk at their feet. But in the gloom of evening and still more at night, the feeling of the place is much more discernable: and there is a sense of evil hanging about like an atmosphere, the lights gleaming round the idols at the far end of a long dim corridor looked like little wicked eyes. It may be imagination, but when I am in the innermost parts of a temple at night I seem to realise more than at any other time or in any other place – except in a temple house itself – the awful tremendous reality of the thing we are up against. 'Oh, God, how long, how long!' is the cry that is forced out of one's heart then. 'Oh that Thou wouldst rend the heavens, that Thou wouldst come down!'

We left the darkened temple courts and stood outside them, but still within the high stone double walls which encircle the whole place; and for fully an hour a group of Brahmin men and lads stood while we told them of the Door opened into the Holiest. It was a wonderful opportunity."

There followed a question and answer session, and the men listened respectfully to the answers given. Amy's colleague, Pappamal, then whispered to Amy, "May I speak?" It was not customary for an Indian woman to speak to men, but Amy, being sure the men in question would be equally respectful to Pappamal, let her go ahead. She told them of her father, a Hindu poet, and of how he too had trusted in the ceremony of the Opening Door, till he found the always-open Door. They gave the men some books and came away.

Later Amy got into a Temple House, without realising it. A little girl of ten was singing to a packed room, and a blind boy was playing in the usual low monotone. Amy, who had entered the room with Christian witness in mind, was waiting for her opportunity. "Presently the child tired," she explained, "and we had our chance. It was perfectly delightful. They let us chant over and over again to an Indian tune the words we wanted to impress on their minds – my favourite way of getting the gospel in – and then, led by the dear old Grandfather, the whole family joined, and chanted it vigorously."

They had some food together, and then the little girl took Amy's hand and said, "Come and see my mother." She went after the child, and found "the old blind grandmother, the child's mother, and a young aunt, such a pretty bright girl; a baby lay asleep in its hammock and a little boy slept on a mat near." They were taken upstairs and were chatting happily when, Amy states,

". . . by chance I noticed the young Aunt's tali (the 'marriage to the god' symbol), and suddenly knew where we were. It was as if a chasm opened at our feet. This great ordinary house was a Temple House, and the old granny was a Temple woman, the child's mother was a Temple woman, the girl was a Temple girl, and the child was a Temple child. When I knew it, I could not speak – it was just too overwhelming. The child, who was sitting between a friend (called D.W. from Palmcottah) and me, with her hands in ours, threw her arms round my neck. "Why do you grieve? It is only that we shall be as you," she said, meaning devoted to the service of God; and then, trying to comfort as she turned first to one then to the other,

her dear little bright face clouded with distress, because we were distressed. Her mother and aunt tried to laugh it off: but soon that mood passed and they seemed concerned, though the effects of their terrible life had seared their power to sympathise. The acuteness of our grief was something utterly beyond them. We left that house feeling broken."

Undaunted – fearless, committed missionary that she was – Amy returned to the Temple House alone the next morning. She records: "It was very unlikely that the mother would see me but she did, and was friendly." Amy sent for a colleague, feeling, "she, being our own, should share this with us. (It had doubly distressed me the night before to plunge one into it who was not ours, and so should not by any conscious act of mine, at any rate, have been exposed to the stinging grief.) Together we sat on the verandah, and watched the baby we would have given so much to carry off with us play with my whistle chain; and the little boy, for whom I have prayed for ten years to be able to start a similar work, stroll in and out with an air of a small, spoilt master of the house; while the mother told me she had paid the little girl's dancing fees (150 rupees), and could not break her promise to the priests. The little girl was called Runji."

Later that day, Amy and her colleagues went to the temple where a crowd had assembled to see the Opening of the Door, which had been shut again after the opening of the day before. Now, with the appointed ceremonial, it had been reopened, and Amy and her friends came in for the last part of it. Her description is worth repeating, for it mightily lays bare her heart and mind:

"The old Jeer, the head priest, a very old man, was standing to receive the homage of the other priests while at intervals music blared and torches were waved before the huge painted idol, the very idol to whom some of our children were to have been given. I thought of them as we stood watching, while the procession formed itself into a long line and moved through the Door, carrying the idol on its shoulders. The semi-darkness was thick with choking dust, there was a confusion of noise, the glare of the red torches waved by the men on either side of that mass of decorated paint lit up the excited faces all around. 'Is it a true god?' I whispered to a little Brahmin girl who held my hand – caste defilement for the day, being in abeyance. 'No!' she whispered back."

Amy then pleads with her prayer supporters: "Now, will you take the child Runji into your deepest memories, and pray and pray and pray? There is no human hope. Then let us hope in God. I cannot tell you how poignant that Temple House episode was. It burnt us. Oh, though your hearts are full of a thousand cares, make room for this one new care. Care for that bright and innocent child. God help you so to care."

So, Amy soldiered on, though the battle was relentless, and the enemy of souls was real. She received great encouragement and blessing from the baptism of two carpenters from Travancore in *the* pool in the Forest. All kinds of complications and stresses had rolled into her life as the project in the Grey Jungle continued. There were setbacks galore, from coolies who stopped working, to walls that started collapsing. Conflict of caste was so great among the workers that, at one stage, the children took over carrying mud, tiles and bricks. Masons huddled in their huts while it rained, and Amy, the children, and Arul Dasan stood in the rain, handing up mats to keep the walls from dissolving. The house, called The Forest House, was finished in 1918. The fact that two men from the Craftsman caste publicly acknowledged their Lord in baptism in *the* pool in the forest, was of great significance. Throughout South India very few Christians were to be found in their caste. As usual, Amy saw a much bigger picture in the smaller one. She writes, "Perhaps the tremendous opposition which marked the building of the Forest House is explained, in part at any rate, by the fact of that breach which was being slowly effected in the walls of that other building, the great Satanic House of Caste. The two men asked to be baptised in the place where they had first heard the gospel. Oh, to have been able to share that day with you."

Amy and lots of the children had 'flu on the occasion of the baptism. She explains:

"We did not look as joyful as we felt, perhaps; and I was glad the Angels were attending to the singing part, for our songs were most croaky. But it was a wonderful day. The Pool looked its very loveliest. A rock runs into the heart of it, and on it one can stand. This rock was coloured a sort of dull gold that day because of the way the light caught it. On either side the water is deep and jade green till it reached the rocks which are grey splashed and veined with crimson, brown, and yellow, and these colours were brokenly reflected in the water. A little waterfall trickled at the further end. This is <u>The Pool</u> of many joyful swimming hours. No photo can show its beauty. If it were not called The Emerald Pool, because of its delicious green, which, however, is softer than emerald, jade is the truer word – it would be called The Water of Laughter. But never was it so happy a pool as that day when those two men confessed Christ Crucified. The toil of the house was as nothing then – the very remembrance fell off. Oh, is there any joy like the joy of such an hour?"

The hideous First World War had now ended, and Dohnavur was not without a special service to mark the occasion.

"Another of our great days was the day we heard of the Armistice. I suppose, the world over, there were groups of gladness on that day. We had a most thrilling little service, with the *Te Deum*, of course, and every praising thing we could find. The school hall was glorious with palms and yellow flowers, and the children were in white and yellow – their Sunday colours. But there was a note of sadness under all. We could never for a moment forget the sorrowing hearts, upon whom the clash of bells must be with an almost agony, and the maimed men in hospitals, blinded or broken for life; and we longed with a longing that hurt, to reach them with our revered affection. Sometimes it seems almost unbearable that we should receive so much and give nothing. What we have to give, is given in certain songs in *Made in the Pans*[1] but will it ever get to any of them?"

Never taking the support she received in times of peace or war for granted, Amy praises her behind-the-scenes friends: "Those who do the behind-the-scenes work of the world are too little known, I think; and I look forward to the time when I shall see them coming in for their share of the joy of harvest. How surprised some of them will be, when they see how God apportions the sheaves."

Let it never be thought that Amy was free from that great 'thorn in the side' of all Christian enterprise: the unspiritual Christian critic. She explained in a *Dohnavur Letter*, "A large new nursery has been built in the field set apart for the Boys Compound. This is the first of the new group of buildings we shall need if we go on growing; and is it possible to stop growing while the children go on Perishing?"

Would such a stirring work escape attack, even from the unspiritual Christian critic? Not so. Amy's scathing response to one of them deserves framing in pure gold: "I had a letter the other day telling me that the writer had no interest in any but evangelistic work. Ours was not that. The 'teaching them to observe all things' of our commission was not Evangelistic, far less so was building. Well, one can't save and then pitchfork souls into Heaven (there are times when I heartily wish we could). And, as for buildings: souls (in India at least) are more or less securely fastened into bodies. Bodies can't be left to lie about in the open, and as you can't get the souls out and deal with them separately, you have to take them both together. What then is to be done?"

The Lord was Amy's shield and her very great reward; and in her letter as well as in her heart she turned away from the critic to God. The Mandarin translation of Isaiah 26 verse 3 is, "You will keep him in perfect peace whose mind stops at God." Amy was proving this truth.

"Had not God," she wrote, "as we reverently believed, directed us to build these buildings? Was the War a surprise to His plans? Must the forces of Hell prevail against Him to the extent of dooming innocent children to perdition? So, we told the masons and carpenters we had a strong and glorious and able God, and that He knew all about the war before it began, and would see us through just as if there was no war: and they took our word for it and went on. And not a man was left unpaid. The thousand pounds came. The second year found us embarked on the last of the six Jewel Nurseries. They cost £100 each. That six hundred pounds came. Every pound of it had a story of its own. I will tell you those stories in Heaven."

She tells of the money coming for the whole Forest project, and the Forest House being built: "Is it not a miracle? And if you could see our Post Office through which the money for the most part comes, if you could see the sordid little muddy mess, the unangelic postmaster, the entirely ordinary nature of everything; above all, if you could see how far we are off the main road of life ('out of sight out of mind', as it would seem), you would realise what a Wonder story I have told you."

She lists the problems the war brought, and explains that at the same time they had experienced famine: "And yet we have been fed, and clothed, and no bills are unpaid today. Oh, that I could sing it all over the world: we have a good Father. It is absolutely safe to trust Him. We may fail, our faith may fail, mine has many a time, and I have had to go to Him desperately for a renewal of it – but He abideth faithful: He cannot deny Himself."

And what next for the faith that faced mountains, and even built a 'Laughing Place' on the side of one? Cholera! In 1919, it raged in the area around Dohnavur. And Amy?

"I sallied forth armed with a pail full of medicines, bottles, tins, rags and disinfectants, which pail was carried by a man coerced for the purpose, for volunteers there were none. I tried hard to get the catechist, a really worthy man (then entirely at loose ends, and I thought badly in need of a job), to see the true nobility of carrying that pail (it was too heavy for me); but he declined. He preferred to carry his Bible, he said, a large book tucked under his arm. He also preferred a prayer meeting to sanitary work. So he would not come. As nobody would, under a big bribe; so I had to give up the useful pail, and either take what I could carry myself or sit by a table in the bungalow verandah and dole out doses to all who came."

She tells of the sadness in the loss of lives, but also records, "Almost all who took our medicines and followed directions, and all those it was possible to nurse, did recover this time in a truly cheering way."

In view of all that she faced, it is difficult not to smile when you read Amy's view of the future beyond 1919: "I believe we here are on the verge of new developments, I see no boundaries to the new horizons out before us." No boundaries? To name but a few of her problems – cholera, child abuse, critics, and the constant care of so many children, she envisaged no boundaries to the development of her work!

In the first *Dohnavur Letter* of 1920, Amy tells of a visit from the Keswick Convention speaker Dr. Charles Inwood to Dohnavur for two days: "It was like our Father to send him for us just at this special time; for of all the old Keswick friends left on earth there is not one other who, because of his own experience, is so fitted to enter into what we are going through, and to give us the food convenient for us, even the very manna of God."

One morning during his stay Amy went with some roses to Dr. Inwood's room. She writes: "He met me with a look of joy on his face. "Amy," he said (how good it is to hear an old friend using the old home name!), "when I was praying this morning the Lord told me to give you £50."" As it happened, there was an immediate need; so the gift was an astonishing solution, and Amy was very grateful. Yet, is there not something deeply moving in reading those words about someone using 'the old home name'? Here was a woman who, in actual fact, had virtually given up her own identity for the sake of India and its need of Christ.

The next development in Amy's work took her in a direction that even her dreams had not revealed. She would find herself identifying deeply with someone who was involved in a social problem of a very different kind.

The Red Tiger

16

IT WAS 1923. From Paris, Coco Chanel convinced the world of women's fashion that even sweaters can be chic, and launched a perfume called Chanel No.5. In the United States, the astronomer, Edwin P. Hubble, discovered a distance-indicating cepheid variable star in the Andromeda nebula; and Colonel Jacob Schick patented the electric razor.

In Munich, as the Nazi party held its first Public Congress, the streets were full of flags and banners displaying the swastika. Herr Hitler's fiery oratory was received with enthusiastic applause. In Germany, a loaf of bread costing 0.63 marks in 1914 was now valued at 201,000,000,000 marks. The currency was valueless.

At Wembley, for the FA Cup Final between Bolton and West Ham, a lone policeman, P.C. George Storey, on his white horse cleared the crowd from the pitch, thus averting a massive disaster. Wembley, designed to hold 100,000, had attracted 201,000 for the occasion. It was feared that a decision to cancel the match would cause mayhem; but, just when the decision seemed inevitable, PC Storey patiently coaxed thousands of very frustrated fans to clear the pitch, and the game was allowed to start. Bolton won 2-0.

In Tokyo, on September 16th, an earthquake razed the city. Two-and-a-half-million people were made homeless, and three hundred-thousand died. In Russia, Lenin also died; and, in India, trouble was brewing when the Council of State, meeting in Allahabad, agreed to restore the Salt Tax. Metaphorically, it was to rub deeply into Indian wounds; but Ghandi soon opposed it in a demonstrably effective way.

On the night of July 11th 1923, Amy Carmichael was to be found in the village of Caruniapuram, staining her arms and face and putting on a dark sari. Around the midnight hour, two men came to her and led her into and through the jungle. At an appointed place, she came face to face with someone whom she had a deep desire to see. He was the most famous outlaw in South India, and he called himself the Red Tiger. His accomplice, Kasi, was almost as famous. Anyone reading English newspapers during the years 1921-23 would have been familiar with their escapades.

Chief of a band of brigands, the Red Tiger (or, Jambulingam – his real name) was a legend. The newspapers dubbed him the Robin Hood of South India, for it was a fact that he robbed the rich and gave most of what he took to the poor. Extremely athletic, he once jumped in excess of twenty feet across a well, catching a Kingfisher in flight at the same time! Raj, as Amy called him, was a crack shot. Once he escaped from Police custody, and sent his guard back with the handcuffs, saying they belonged to the Police Station! He loved children, and was very kind to old people.

What was his story? It was a story of a man who, although he was honest, had been falsely accused; and after his summons arrived he fled from India to Penang. Worried about his wife and children, he returned; only to find that his enemies had been blackening his name to an even darker shade. The police had been terrifying his wife, including the use of physical abuse. So he fled again, this time to the mountains, and his wife died of shock. He believed that he had no chance of justice, because he feared *himsa*. Explaining this problem, Amy wrote, "The Sanskrit word means slaughter, pain, affliction. In the part of the country to which the story refers, the word connotes anything unjust done in the name of justice: physical pain inflicted to extort a confession, blackmail, a false charge in court, the removal of small properties or money, insult in public or private, vexation, rudeness. The exact shade of meaning is determined by the context." We would call it Corruption in the Legal System.

Raj saw no point in facing the charge against him and trying to prove his innocence. The police were often corrupt, or easily deceived by false evidence. They accepted that version of a story as being true, from the person who offered them the biggest bribe. False witnesses were paid well by the false accusers. Eventually, though, Raj gave himself up at a Police Station. To him, *himsa* meant, first, flogging; then molten wax being dropped on his foot; then came 'nail and hammer' *himsa*. This involved the foot being held down, and a nail or strong thorn being put upon the root of the toe-nail and tapped smartly with a small hammer. Sometimes, a hot brick was pressed between the hands, which were tied behind the back, and then needles were pressed into the quick of a nail. There was an Indian proverb for this: "the pointing finger must be cut off." There was also the '20 needle' *himsa*; or another method they used to extract a confession was when red hot wire was passed into the ear; or sometimes it could mean that a person's feet were often tied to a beam while the head was held over the smoke of a fire into which chillies had been thrown.

Amy wrote later:

"It is possible to do *himsa* without producing signs of injuries on the body. There are haunting illusions in the common speech of the people that have not sprung ready-made from the dust . . . 'the man who sets himself to track an age-old wrong to its lair will not walk on primroses, but will walk barefoot on flints and stinging thorns.' 1,300 miles from the corner of India to which Raj's story belonged, a young Police Officer came to his Chief with the truth about these matters. 'It will be hell, but I'll stand by you,' said that Officer, who was high in his profession and keen to combat evil. The lad could not face it. He went home and shot himself."

Raj's obstinacy when suffering his torture angered his examiner, and he hit him on the face with his sandal. Fury rose in him, and Raj escaped before they could get him safely to the district jail. He became in name what he was not by character: a criminal and an outlaw. He never robbed at night, believing it to be wrong, but robbed during the day – it was 'daylight robbery', as far as Raj was concerned! Of course, it was not long before the story of Raj reached the ears of the Wild-bird Child. She later stated that she was filled with a strong desire, "to take this brigand chief by the hand, and lead him to the Saviour of Men." Of course, it seemed impossible; "but," she wrote, "in God's great dictionary that word does not occur." Later she wrote, "He had no god; nor demon, nor devil, nor godling, nor goddess," to whom he could turn. Yet, for Amy, no one – but no one – was outside the reach of God's love, not even Raj. Could she see him? Could she tell him of that love? She asked, of course, but it was thought to be impossible. Did she not know the God of the Impossible? So she talked with Him about the problem.

Then the impossible happened: God gave Raj the desire to meet Amy Carmichael! She was up at the Grey Jungle overseeing some building work, and for eight evenings Raj and his men secretly watched her. Then, on an October evening in 1921, one legend was waylaid by another. Amy had come with two others to view some land near the foothills, when Raj and his men stepped out from behind a rock and greeted her. Raj told her who he was. One wonders if Amy Carmichael ever got 'goose pimples' when a prayer was answered so dramatically in front of her eyes? On the other hand, did she ever shiver with fear? What did she do? She offered them tea and bread out of her basket, and they sat down and ate it. Then the others left Amy and Raj alone, as Raj poured out his story. There can have been few stories that Amy Carmichael ever heard equal to that one, to arouse her keen sense of drama.

"But what about your three children?" asked the woman with a mother's heart. "Would you take them at Dohnavur?" asked the outlaw. "Of course," Amy replied. "I promise to welcome them." Amy urged him to surrender to the Superintendent of the Police, but he feared *himsa*. She did extract one promise from him: he promised never again to use his gun, except in the defence of his life.

The missionary heart of Amy Carmichael now rose to the challenge; and, at the foothills of that Indian jungle, she told the outlaw of the Saviour. A Saviour, when we think about it, who Himself actually suffered *himsa* in the form of false witnesses, and torture beyond words: *His visage was marred more than any man's, and His form more than the sons of men* (Isaiah 52:14). That same Saviour, of course, had also saved the dying thief. They all knelt together in prayer. The heart that empathised with the poor lady on a Belfast street decades before, still beat with the same compassion.

Five days following that meeting in the Grey Jungle, Raj and his men were lured into a trap, tortured, and then taken to hospital under guard. No sooner did Amy hear the news but she was off to the hospital. Raj was truly glad to see her, and she him. When he was transferred to the district jail, he studied the Bible that Amy had given to him. A beautiful verse in Deuteronomy 32:10, that she had marked, spoke volumes to him: *He found him in a desert land, and in the waste howling wilderness; he led him about, he instructed him, he kept him as the apple of his eye.* Let no one say that God's Word is not relevant.

One day when Amy was visiting him, he pulled out a copy of John Bunyan's *Pilgrim Progress* from under his pillow, with a picture of the burden of sin falling from Pilgrim's back. He told Amy, "It's like that with me: my burden has been loosed, it has fallen from me." The man had been converted!

There can be no doubt or argument that God spoke to Amy Carmichael in her dreams. In January 1922, she was in the Grey Jungle again, and one night she dreamt that she was outside the gates of the jail. The gates opened with no delay, and she went straight to the hospital ward where Raj lay. She asked him, "Do you want to be baptised?" "Yes," he said; "When?" she asked; "Now," he replied. Then she was aware of a missionary passing by, and she asked him to go and baptise Raj. He did so, giving him the name 'Jewel of Prayer.'

It happened exactly as she had dreamt. On January 30th 1922, she arrived at the jail. The Superintendent was just about to enter, so the gate opened without Amy having to say a word. She asked Raj the questions, and he answered her as in her dream. She then asked him to write a statement explaining his wish to be baptised, and the Superintendent initialled it. That evening a missionary, passing by on his way from Calcutta to Palmcottah, was met by Amy, and he agreed to baptise Raj. So Raj and Kasi were baptised the very next morning by the Rev. E. A. L. Moore, who later became Bishop of Travancore and Cochin.

When one considers the seeming impossibility of an Irish woman missionary helping to lead a notorious Indian outlaw to personal faith in Jesus Christ, and to see him baptised while yet in prison, one is challenged that far too often we, who have spiritual light, hide it 'under a bushel.' The result is that those who need it most, are deprived of it.

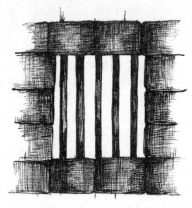

Raj pleaded guilty at his trial. However, after hearing the story of Peter's miraculous escape from prison, read to him by a Tamil clergyman, the comparatively untaught Raj decided to make a break for it! He, Kasi, and two others escaped, and for a year they returned to their outlaw existence, although they never actually robbed again.

Life is never simple. Poor Amy was now caught between a rock and a hard place, regarding Raj and his men. Eyebrows were raised among some British officials; and they were not altogether certain that Amy was not to blame for the situation. She turned again to prayer, and had cause to be thankful that Raj did not retaliate against those who had betrayed him. He refused to steal again, but other robbers used his name. When the authorities came to believe that Raj was robbing again, they called Amy to Palmcottah, to meet one or two British officials. She pledged that Raj was living honestly and was not robbing, but they were totally unconvinced.

Through intermediaries, Amy got in touch with the men, and urged them to trust the British authorities, and surrender. Night after night in December 1922 she kept a light burning, in the hope that they might do just that. To complicate things, a number of men from the village of Caruniapuram that was situated near Raj's home, inspired by the amazing change in Raj, professed to have become Christians. Some of them came to Dohnavur asking for protection!

Eventually, Amy was approached by an important official, who tried to get her to persuade Raj and his men to come in. So, that is the reason why, on the night of July 11th 1923, Amy stained her face and arms, put on her sari, and was led and carried into the jungle for an arranged meeting with the notorious outlaw. Led eventually to the rendezvous by an imitated bird call and answering whistle, Amy records that, when she arrived, Raj and Kasi took her hands and "fondled them as children would a mother's."

As they talked and Amy again pled that they should surrender, it became clear that the men felt it was too late. They admitted the stupidity of their escape from prison. Fearing that they would die with blood on their hands, Amy bravely stated, "If only I heard that you had died without a weapon in your hand, I could bear it." "Do not fear," said Raj. "Will God forsake us?" They prayed, and it was truly a sorrowful parting.

In her *Dohnavur Letter* of July 14th 1923, Amy gave her supporters some of the background to the story, and it helps to put the whole situation into proper perspective. She refers to Raj as Robin, as in *Robin Hood*. "Not a crumb was laid to his charge at that time, and the police, who haunted us with the idea that I could wave a wand and bring him in, told me that he must be entirely changed, which was good hearing."

She writes, "A campaign of false charges began, engineered, as we who live in the midst of these matters knew, by an official who for reasons of his own preferred Robin to stay out." She points out that, newspapers "publish lurid columns on the activities of the Indian Robin Hood, as they still call him." The story was copied in the English, Irish, Scottish and Australian papers. (One wonders what they would have thought of it down in Millisle!) She tells her supporters that three hundred men, under two Englishmen, are soon to join forces. Aided by hunting dogs, their intention is to track down her child-in-the-faith. Significantly, in the midst of all the complications of the unravelling story ("His affairs will persist in mixing themselves up with everything; and I can't disentangle them"), Amy records the spiritual blessings that followed Raj's conversion to Christ. She writes of a village under the mountains, where the relatives of Raj and Kasi lived:

"The Lord our God has been working. I am just back from the village, and feel as if I had been in a dream place. It is not like India. It is like a story, or a dream. Six months ago some poor tormented men fled from that village to us for refuge. The police (please remember this is India) were trying to force them, by torture and by threats of false charges, to catch Robin, or betray him to them. This, as they knew he was living straight, they refused to do."

Amy sheltered the men, and told the Police Superintendent that she had done so. They worked in the field for their food and, Amy notes, ". . . better work was never done in it." The men believed the gospel and turned to the Lord. One of them was baptised – the first in his village, and "a vibrant, live little church was founded in their area." One can only imagine Amy's joy in the spiritual harvest, following her sowing in the heart of an outlaw. While facing stinging criticism from various quarters for what she had done, she was able to describe truthfully the spiritual life that resulted in the planting of that little church. She writes:

"The singing . . . the throb of life, oh, it was most joyful. And God said, 'Let there be light, and there was light.' It was like that ... until then the village had been darkness itself. Not a Christian had been allowed a foot in there . . . There was one who 14 years ago had wanted to be a Christian, but his father beat him and led him to a pillar and he gave in. He was the first to be baptised. Will someone focus on that father? He is a fine old man, tall, good looking, well-off (hence his chief handicap), and entirely uninterested. To be a Christian means honest weights and measures, and his merchandise would lose by it. He is a landowner and sells palm sugar. Pray for him."

Amy describes the people's fear, as the overlord threatens to bring false charges against them, in connivance with the police. She writes of a lad she calls 'Courage'. "Such a fine lad he was, thrashed to make him bare false witness, and beaten about the face with a round office-ruler until the blood came, but he never yielded." In November 1923, she records nineteen adult baptisms and six children from that village.

Amy used the conversion of Raj and his changed life to speak to others. After a visit to the place of recent spiritual blessing, she writes:

"In our little village on the far away mountain, the people were bowed down in penitence, men and women prayed for pardon for their sins. The guidance was often delightful; I was tired after what seemed a vain walk in the sun, and suddenly there was the sound of a blow, and I saw a child being beaten by a great man. 'This child says He, whom he calls Jesus, can alone save from sin,' explained the man who had struck the little lad. The boy looked up bravely, thinking he was going to be struck again; but instead he heard to his relief a loving invitation to the angry man to listen to his story. And the story of Jesus, Saviour of sinners – Saviour of the Robber Captain, of whom of course he had heard, held that angry man entranced. At last, 'Come,' he said to the little boy – 'come back to my village, and tell me more about your God,' and they went on together."

One of the men from the village was called 'Christudas'. Amy describes him as a priceless gift, "who has taken over all the land matters, and manages the out-of-door men servants at Dohnavur." She reminds her supporters that she is responsible for seven hundred vegetable meals a day that had to be cooked. "You can imagine what the burden of field and kitchen garden can be; we have searched for years for a man of this type, but could never find one. He is one of the many gifts (whose inner value no one understands as we do) given to us in connection with the long, hard fight for the soul of the one-time robber captain."

On September 20th 1923, Raj and Kasi were lured to a feast in Caruniapuram. It was a trap: the house in which the feast was held was surrounded by the police. Raj and Kasi fired from the windows, and wounded two of the police. When the police set fire to the thatched roofs of the surrounding houses, Raj and Kasi made a break for it. As they crossed the stream Kasi slipped, and the police shot him. Raj ran on, totally unaware that his friend had been gunned down, and then turned to wait for him coming. The wait sealed his death. Friends later reported that he sprang on to a bank of red earth. Then it looked as if he had remembered something, and swinging his gun three times around his head he threw it away. Raj then tore his white scarf from his shoulders and, standing bare to his waist, he shouted, "You, whose duty it is to shoot, shoot here!" – pointing to his heart. They shot, but missed. He then looked to Heaven and, raising his hands in worship, walked slowly backwards and stood under a tarimund tree. Facing his parents' graves to the west he did obeisance, and returned to the tree and now stood with his back against the trunk. The police fired again – sixteen bullets went into the bark behind him, and more into the branches above him, and the sand beneath him. He was unscathed. When he sank slowly, as though to kneel, the police pounced on him. Disgusting though it is to report, one of them bit into Raj's neck in order to drink the blood of such a courageous man. Another policeman broke his arm. The police then dragged him towards the water, where one of their number shot Raj through the head at point blank range. The Red Tiger moved no more.

On hearing the news of the death of her friend, Amy's immediate reaction was to ask a question: "Had they sinned?" "No," replied the bearer of the sad news, "they died clean."

Amy suffered serious criticism, even in high places, for her friendship with Raj and his men. She had dared once more to venture into sensitive territory for the Lord's sake, where the lines between the law and a soul's need clashed. A Hindu book was actually written by a Hindu author, for Hindus using fictitious names, telling of the change in the Robber Captain. The social reformer within Amy, though, rose to the challenge; and she decided to write a book about it herself, entitled *Raj, Brigand Chief*. Its target was the horrendous practice of *himsa*, and corruption within the legal system. She secured forewords for her book from the Bishops of Travancore, Tirunelveli and Madras, and a missionary surgeon. When preparing the book, Amy held it back for quite a time, in order to verify all her facts. In a very powerful way, she uncovered the corruption that everyone knew of, but few would speak out against. Her uncompromising commitment to the truth had wide social, as well as spiritual, implications. Eventually the book was translated into other languages, including Persian, Arabic, and some European languages, including, it seems, Yiddish. Again, a missionary matter had become a national, if not an international, matter.

At the close of all his letters to Amy, Raj had written, "Emmanuel, my help." As Christmas 1923 settled upon Dohnavur, the awesome truth of *Emmanuel, God with us* could not have been more poignant.

The Unbound Christ

17 IT WAS 1928. On January 16th Thomas Hardy, the novelist and poet, was buried beside Charles Dickens in Westminster Abbey. Kipling, Barrie, Galsworthy, Shaw, Gosse and Houseman were his Pallbearers. On March 29th the Suffragettes' long campaign finally came to an end, as the House of Commons overwhelmingly passed the Equal Franchise Bill, giving the vote to all women aged twenty-one or over. Emily Pankhurst, the famous Suffragette leader, died.

In April, Chinese National Troops launched a long-expected offensive, with the ultimate aim of capturing the capital, Peking. The Norwegian explorer, Ammundsen, died in June, when his seaplane crashed during an Arctic rescue attempt. In July, King Fuad became the new dictator of Egypt, and Walt Disney's Mickey Mouse made his first appearance in the sound-film, *Steamboat Willie*. Elastoplast sticking plaster was first manufactured in Hull, England. By October, in the ninth year of Prohibition, bootleg whiskey, contaminated with wood, had claimed five hundred and eighteen lives in New York, thirty-three in one week. In India, the Nationalist, Pandit Nehru, called for rebellion if India did not get Dominion status by the end of the year.

At the beginning of the year, it was decided that the time had come to think about purchasing land for a hospital at Dohnavur. It was agreed to call the hospital *Parama Suha Salai*, the 'Place of Heavenly Healing.' The name was the suggestion of a Brahman friend from a local town, who had received medical help in Dohnavur when the doctors were running a small dispensary there, before the hospital was built. In August 1929, the members of *The Dohnavur Fellowship* were called together for a time of prayer. On the basis of 1 John 5:14-15, they asked the Lord for £10,000 for Parama Suha Salai, as it was felt that this was what would be needed for the project. The first £1,000 gift for the hospital arrived on the day before Amy's sixty-second birthday. The building of the hospital was spread over many years, and most of the money came from small gifts. The children themselves contributed in all sorts of small ways. The hospital provided private kitchens for each patient's family. As Murray Webb-Peploe stated, it was to be a place, "where people may come, not to be preached at, dosed, and dealt with as cases, but to feel at home, to watch, to thaw, to allow those who take their names and wash their bandages and dress their wounds to share with them what the Lord Jesus Christ has done and can do for them."[1]

Alongside this project, another beautiful project emerged. It was called *The House of Prayer*. An old Indian carpenter gave two months' pay for what became a vital place of worship for the Dohnavur Family. He thought it all wrong that, while almost innumerable temples and shrines were found everywhere around him, the Dohnavur Fellowship had no place of worship. *The Dohnavur Fellowship* prayed for the money required to complete the work, and the children contributed magnificently, sending Amy notes telling her they wouldn't waste soap, spill milk or oil. They got involved in digging and in carrying lime and sand. The lovely building was eventually finished, and stands to this day in the centre of the compound at Dohnavur.

A gift was earmarked *for a Prayer Tower*. The roof of the building has two pointed shafts – a symbol of the unity of the spiritual and the secular in the life of holiness. Every morning and evening a hymn is played on the bells; and every hour the bells ring for a moment of stillness for prayer and reflection. There is a floor of polished red tiles, and no furniture except for a few chairs for the sick and elderly, and foreigners who have not yet mastered the art of sitting on a floor. In the services, children still wave coloured flags during the singing of certain songs, as Amy instituted; for she wisely knew how hard it is for children to sit inactive. Across the years, older folk have accompanied the singing with bells, cymbals, triangles, tambourines, and clay pot drums with a leather flap over the mouth. The House of Prayer is not a place to sleep. Thanksgiving Services and three services every Sunday are held here, one in English and two in Tamil. The singing from those hundreds of bare-footed children is 'something else'. Communion Services were also instituted. A House of Prayer and a Place of Heavenly Healing: it was a beautiful combination. It was all in answer to *tide*-prayers, not *wave*-prayers. The explanation of such prayers is to be found in a poem, included in the November 1928 *Dohnavur Letter*:

Lord Jesus, Intercessor,
Oh, teach us how to pray;
Not wave-like, rising, falling
In fitful clouds of spray.
The mighty tides of ocean
A deeper secret know,
Their currents undefeated move
Whatever winds may blow.

Lord Jesus, Intercessor,
Creator of the sea,
Teach us the tide's great secret
Of quiet urgency.
Spindrift of words we ask not,
But, Lord, we seek to know
The conquering patience of the tides,
Whatever winds may blow

After long years of travelling by bullock bandy, Amy was very grateful for the combustion engine.

"Can you imagine what it is," she wrote, "to have the Ford and the lorry so that hundreds of children and dear hard-working girls might be taken to the sea? I wish I could copy out their sea letters, 'the sea sends you his vast love' is the way Tara's latest ends. Not all have been there yet, but all will go and we bless most comprehensively the givers of Joppa. The Ford and the lorry and the Forest House and all the other good things which refresh the outworn, and make the childhood of these children something joyful to look back upon while memory lasts."

In February 1930, down at Travancore, owing to a recent visit of the Viceroy there were large amounts of electrical machinery and stores going cheap. All were in first class condition, as they had only been used for special illuminations during the two nights of the Viceroy's stay. On a visit to a large English Electrical Company in Madras, Amy was offered two special generators that had been specially tested and supplied from England for the Viceroy's visit. They were practically brand new. Would she take them? "I told them that I would write my answer; I would have to put the matter before the Fellowship on my return." She then states, "I went out, had lunch somewhere, did a lot of thinking and praying and then guidance came, clear as a shot, 'buy them'. She went sharply back to the Electrical Company, closed on the offer, and bought them. "Next morning," she continues, "I got a letter from the Manager of the Electrical firm – 'You will be interested to know that at 4.00 p.m. this afternoon we received a telegraphic order for the engines from another party, so you did well yesterday in deciding to have them.'"

On May 16th 1930, Dohnavur got its first electric light. Amy comments, "It is a marvel that never gets less marvellous." As for electric fans, "that turn solemnly round as though alive, the children stand and gaze. It is a wonderful world, they think; and so it is." The current generated was used to give light where it was needed for community use, e.g. the House of Prayer, the hospital operating theatre, etc. The houses did not get electric light until the 1950's, when the newly-independent Indian Government constructed hydro-electric schemes in the mountains that brought light and power to the villages. Amy's love for her children continued unabated; no different from the day, 30 years before, when little Preena first walked on to her verandah at Dohnavur, and then right into her heart.

As Christmas 1930 approached, the experience of asking for blue eyes in Millisle, Co. Down sixty years before, was still fresh in her heart. In December 1930, she quotes the words of her famous poem about her childhood experience of asking for blue eyes: "I find the *Dohnavur Letter* goes to quite a number of people who have kept the heart of the child. And more than one of that sort here has found an answer to many a question in the last line of this song – the question that answers itself. As for the genuine child, it never tires of the nonsense of it. We have baby song evenings in my room sometimes, and Godfrey plays on his auto-harp and the children crowd round with their own little Baby Song M.S. books. What shall we sing? *Blue Eyes*! they cry all at once, and with emphasis – so just to share our nonsense as well as our sense, here it is. . . " She includes not only the words of her poem but the music to sing it as a song.

In 1931, a call went out to all the members of *The Donhavur Fellowship*, to gather in God's Garden at Dohnavur. There the decision was made to ask Murray and Godfrey Webb-Peploe to be the leaders of the men's work at Dohnavur; and Dr. May Powell to be the leader of the women's work. At sixty-three, Amy was looking to the future. After years of pressure, trial, grief, and huge responsibilities, her health was showing the strain. She was very tired, exhausted even, and had multiple arthritis, which Dr. Robbins believes was the cause of a lot of neuritic pain in her right arm and hand, which made it difficult for Amy to write or hold a book to read. Did this mean that her spiritual vision for the work slackened? Not in the slightest. At a special gathering held one evening in August 1931, she was concerned for what she called 'the Great Undone'. Based on Isaiah 54:2, they asked that there might be a 'lengthening of cords', a 'strengthening of stakes'. The log-book reads: "Funds short, the very time to look for an advance . . . great joy tonight in the sense of moving on together." For Amy, though, her advance was to come from twenty-one years of incredible restriction, and her strengthening from a place of great weakness.

In 1926, Amy and some colleagues went to a town called Kalakadu, about four miles from Dohnavur. Finding a drama company about to make a presentation, Amy approached the Manager and got permission to take to the stage and tell the story of the Lord Jesus. A week later, she and her colleagues went back. Ronald Proctor and Amy gave an advertised public lecture on *The Great War in Mesopotamia*; and the story of *Raj the Brigand*. From this, they illustrated the gospel story to the crowd. The players were about to follow, and blazing lights surrounded the stage. (I'd have given anything to be there, as Amy held forth on her story of her friend, the outlaw!) It was a town where there was no willingness to listen to the gospel. Five years later a break came, when a house in the town was offered to the Dohnavur Fellowship for rent. They were warned that there was a curse on the place, and it was haunted. Nevertheless, the house was taken for a dispensary.

In the early morning of October 24th 1931, Amy talked to the Lord and prayed this prayer: "Do with me as Thou wilt. Do *anything*, Lord, that will fit me to serve Thee and help my beloveds." In the afternoon she was driven to the house in Kalakadu, as she wanted to ensure that all was in order for the women who were to work in the house. The key could not be found immediately, and it was twilight before it was obtained. Amy went to an outside toilet, a newly erected palm-leaf shed. The builders had dug the borehole just inside the door, instead of at the back where it should have been. In the darkness Amy did not see it, and fell across the opening of the narrow pit, twisting her spine, breaking her leg, and dislocating an ankle. In much pain, she was taken by lorry to the hospital at Neyyoor, forty-six miles away, on what became a wild, stormy night, with downpouring rain.

Amy returned to Dohnavur on November 3rd 1931, and much prayer arose for her. Everyone wished her a speedy recovery. On Christmas Eve, carols were sung outside her room, and she appeared on the verandah. Dr. Howard Somervell, who took care of her, told her she would walk again in time. However, Amy was never to walk far again. She did walk about her house a little until 1948, when she fell in her bathroom and broke the neck of her femur. In truth, however, she was to be an invalid for the remaining twenty-one years of her life.

In 1919, she had added a note to one of her *Dohnavur Letters*. Its truth was perfectly apposite to her life:

"And now, though I am very loath to inflict anything on any who don't care for such things (but won't such, please, skip) I have a longing to reach some unknown unselfish people who, invalided or otherwise handicapped yet bear us up, and fight alongside in a hundred ways. I know of some such but not all, and this is for them (the story I should perhaps say is forty years old – forty years ago a certain very homesick child was sent to a Boarding School, where the only comforting thing was a tall lily who stood in the terribly long and formal dining room).

She grew, a plant of fair renown,
Where other lilies be;
They saw her white and golden crown,
And never more was she
Among the lilies of the wood,
For they that plucked her thought it good
That in another kind of room
That lily-flower should bloom.

And to that room one day there came
A little wild-bird child
But lately caught, and nowise tame,
And all unreconciled
To cages and to careful bars
That seemed to ban the very stars;
The lily looked at her and smiled,
As though herself a child.

And their eyes met, no word was said
That man could hear or say,
But thus the child was comforted;
And after, flown away
To far, far lands, remembering this,
A comfort it were loss to miss,
Would even in this later hour
Sing joy to some dear flower.

O whosoe'er ye be, and where,
However straitly bound,
Your ministry is as the air
That sails the whole world round.
Do ye but fill your present room
With sweetness as of heavenly bloom,
Ye know not where it may be found:
Is Christ within you bound?

Oh it is true – ye know not where it may be found, that gift, that prayer, that loving, loving letter – for the Unbound Christ in you was in it."

Though Amy was to be an invalid for the next twenty-one years, as we shall see the risen Christ within her was not to be bound in her life either.

Dust Of Gold

18   IT WAS March 1947. The great-granddaughter of the nineteenth century philanthropist, Lord Shaftesbury, and daughter of the Jewish-born Sir Ernest Cassell, Edwina, Lady Mountbatten, turned to go through the door that led out to the Mogul Garden. Edwina, now the Vicereine of India, had been strolling in the garden with Mahatma Gandhi and her husband the Viceroy, Lord Mountbatten.

A point in history was approaching, that was extremely delicate in every way. In August, India, with its four hundred million people – one-quarter of the world's population – was to be delivered up by the British to the Indians. The great question of the hour was whether Britain would be able to hand over a united India, or an India divided in two – Muslim and Hindu. Every available newsman and photographer was on hand to observe and record the confrontation between these two very contradictory figures who had met for a two-hour talk. They had not expected Edwina to be present. The stroll in the garden of the Viceroy's residence had been taken as 'a breather' in the talks, and given as a photo-opportunity to the eager photographers.

As the three central figures in the drama hurried to go in again, Gandhi was seen to place his hand trustingly on Edwina's right shoulder. That defining moment was captured by the American photographer, Max Desfors, and within a very few days people right across the earth saw it and took heart.

Let it be recorded again that Edwina carried out incredible work in the last, raw, frightening, anguished days of the British Raj. As riot victims increased to thousands a day, her unremitting relief work was outstanding. There were fewer nurses in all-India than in all-London. On May 23rd the British Cabinet agreed to Lord Mountbatten's proposal for the partition of India into two states, one Muslim and the other Hindu. Edwina's tours of devastated areas, comforting the homeless, grief-stricken people, were far removed from the work of former Vicereines. She did not draw back from the dirt, stench, fatigue, danger and disease, or from horrendously gruesome scenes. She would return grey with weariness from the work and heat, in temperatures of up to one hundred and fourteen degrees Fahrenheit. She had what has been described as near-frenzied concern for the sufferings of India, with its plagues and pestilence.

Edwina need not have become so involved; she could have protected herself at the Viceroy's residence in Delhi, with its State rooms, drawing rooms, and bedrooms with their slow-turning ceiling fans, and immaculately dressed servants. She could have driven in style along Delhi's broad avenues, designed by the brilliant Lutyens, or gone often to the cool Vice Regal lodge at Simla. Instead, after Independence, as Delhi itself became a refugee camp, Edwina achieved the superb feat of uniting fifteen organisations under the banner of the United Council of Relief and Welfare. Her husband's ADC's were very nervous of going out with her: she would stop in the middle of sniping to pick up bodies and take them to the local infirmaries. One incident in particular is intriguing. It says a lot about Edwina, around whose heels scandal and selfishness had long snapped, and had sometimes been embraced.

Freedom for India came at midnight on August 14th 1947, when one hundred and sixty-three years of British rule ended. The celebrations of Independence Day followed, when an estimated six hundred thousand people gathered near the war memorial in Princes

Park for the unfurling of the national flag. Indira Gandhi records that, because of the crowds and the crush, Lord Mountbatten was not able to hoist the flag, so he was forced to hoist it from a large distance, with tied strings. She records that at one moment a mother could find no other place for her baby that looked safe, except in the arms of Edwina (now Countess Mountbatten). "She smiled and held the baby tight." Marie Seton, a biographer, stated, "to my mind, but for the dynamic, flexible cement supplied by Edwina, I can't imagine how a blood-bath *vis-à-vis* all India and Britain could have been avoided, much less a republic within the Commonwealth achieved. It was an incredible transformation."

Independence Day passed off quietly in the Dohnavur compound. In the village they had some fireworks and chorused shouting of 'Victory to India'. In the Dohnavur compound they had a simple talk about the change of Government, and then the new flag of India was raised. They all stood around it and prayed for the country. It was, in fact, a time of great turmoil on the subcontinent. By the end of December 1947, it was estimated that four hundred thousand people, both Muslims and Hindus, had been slaughtered since the partition of the old India, five months previously. A further one hundred thousand had suffered cruelly from starvation and exposure. Official figures announced that more than eight million refugees, almost equally divided between Hindu and Muslim, had crossed the Indo-Pakistan border, in what was then the largest migration of people in history. The majority had to fight their way through hostile country in bullock cart convoys, under frequent attack. The world's largest democracy had a difficult birth; its survival, constant growth, and amazing comparative stability into the twenty-first century is one of the most incredible political stories of all time.

Gandhi wanted the British to walk out of India; and, in the end, that is what they did. Their departure, though, did not in the least affect Amy Carmichael's commitment to India. She believed that any furlough from her work would have been an 'exile'.

In the years since her fall at Kalakadu, Amy was for the most part an invalid who rarely left her room. The expected healing, after a few weeks of rest, did not materialise. The strain of thirty-eight years' incredible commitment in the 'war of the Lord' went deeper than even Amy realised. She endured a lot of pain, in the days when pain-killing drugs were not so readily available as they are now. Her activities were confined mainly to one room; and yet those years of confinement brought an even greater ministry, which was truly international in its impact.

Amy kept a large aviary on her verandah, into which she placed beautiful birds. At times she would let them free in her room, much to the frustration of her nurses. She wrote:

What a God, who out of shade
Nest for singing bird hath made.
Lord, my Might and Melody,
I will sing to Thee.

The Wild-bird child sang a song, which was to be heard by millions. Godfrey Webb-Peploe wrote the *Dohnavur Letter* for a time; but eventually the busy leader was allowed to lay it aside; and Amy took on the responsibility for writing a new series of letters, called *Dust of Gold*. She continued to write the major part of it until 1948. The title was based on a passage from the Book of Job: *As for the earth, from it comes bread, but underneath it is turned up as by fire; Its stones are the source of sapphires, and it contains gold dust* (Job 28:5-6). Amy explained its purpose to her readers thus:

"One of the chiefest joys to me in writing to you is that it gives a chance for all those tiny things that some I know want to hear. I am glad I found the name *Dust of Gold*; for if anyone says 'Oh but these are such trifles, most unsuitable for a missionary letter,' I can say, 'well then, the letter is true to its name. Dust doesn't profess to be boulders. You needn't read it at all, if you have a soul above dust.'"

In the February–June 1933 edition she writes, "The love of my most beloved family . . . has been beyond telling. And love is the heavenliest thing I know. It is like music, like beauty, not of earth at all. Love is of God. God is Love. I feel like a baby just learning to spell these words. These nineteen months have been spent in that blessed spelling class." In the June 1933–February 1934 issue of *Dust of Gold*, Amy placed a little story on the front page. It read: "In 355BC Philip of Macedon, father of Alexander the Great, took away the ladders up which his soldiers had swarmed onto the ramparts of a strong Greek city, thus making retreat impossible." That little story represents Amy's attitude to the commitment of her calling. There was no retreat.

The needs of Dohnavur were as great as ever, and God was faithful. In August 1934 she wrote, "The God who sends the daffodils will not forget the corn." She pointed out, "We use one thousand two hundred sacks of rice a year, and, as the bullock carts trundle slowly past the low wall which borders my garden, I have counted the long carts in wonder and thanksgiving."

Dust of Gold was no tame publication. One issue reveals Amy storming against the practice of the inhumane killing of animals for sacrifice. She does not spare her readers the gruesome details, nor the sadistic attitude of people to the suffering animals. "Laws will not end these things," she cries. "The Sarda law, forbidding marriage before a girl is 14 and a boy 18, is the joke of jokes. India does not even pretend to obey it."

As Amy's pen, and now more often her pencil, got busy, an outstanding creativity began to flow. Above the door outside her room, on light teakwood in sepia, was written, *The Room of Peace*.

From that room, after her fall in October 1931, she wrote thirteen books, thousands of personal letters, and hundreds of songs and poems. She also wrote daily notes to those near to her at Dohnavur. During this period her books included *Gold Cord*, which was the story of Dohnavur. It linked its extraordinary history together in one volume, and gave the inside story of *The Dohnavur Fellowship*. It was published in 1932. Then came *Rose from Brier*, intended only for those who were ill, which appeared in 1933. It began as letters to the ill; in its book form it is still ministering wisdom, insight, spiritual truth and cheer to sick people across the world. There is something very real, when a person who is ill writes to people who are also ill. It is not mere theory. As Amy put it:

> The toad beneath the harrow knows
> Exactly where each tooth-point goes.
> The butterfly upon the road
> Preaches contentment to that toad.

In 1934 came *Ploughed Under*, the story of a little lover. It was the story of her colleague, Arulai. Her purpose in writing the book was to show, ". . . the way of the Lover of Souls with the soul that He calls to Himself." Amy once stated, "In moonlight nothing is uninteresting;" so, in 1935, came *Gold by Moonlight*, for those who walk in difficult places. It brought a lot of appreciative mail. *Toward Jerusalem*, a little book of verse, came in 1936; and *Windows*, a story of provision, in 1937. One of Amy's most thought-provoking books came in 1938, and was simply called *If*. It was short and pithy, just a few sentences in each page; but it powerfully revealed what was entailed in having 'Calvary love'. *Figures of the True* came in 1938; and in the same year *Pools and the Valley of Vision*. The latter was for all those who love water, and expressively reveals the comfort and inspiration Amy absorbed, in the midst of a hectic life, from deep pools and running water. The story of Kohila, the child for whom Amy risked jail, came in 1939. Then, in 1941, she wrote *His Thoughts Said . . . His Father Said*, a little book somewhat in the same mode as *If*. It is a book that aims to correct emotional and unbalanced thinking with Biblical thinking.

Do Amy Carmichael's books and her life still have influence? Who could calculate the impact of her life? In my little world, I was recently dining with my family at the Royal County Down Golf Club, at the kind invitation of a member. The member's daughter, a Cambridge University graduate who has recently been involved in establishing a Christian school in England, asked me what I was writing at the moment. "A life of Amy Carmichael," I answered. "I called my daughter after Amy," she said quietly. "I have read most of her books." I can honestly tell you that I did not expect to find Amy Carmichael's influence at a dinner table in the Royal County Down!

One has only to study the lives and works of people like Dr. Billy Graham's wife, Ruth; or the outstanding writer and missionary, Elizabeth Elliot, to see what influence Amy's books have had. In Northern Ireland, where I live, children in Primary Schools study from a unique and unprecedented resource. The inter-board religious education project for Key Stage Two is on the life of Amy Carmichael. It is based on an inter-church agreed syllabus, and children just love it. "I didn't like it when Amy's life activity was over," one child wrote; and another boy commented, "I learned that NO is an answer."[3] The study is a fascinating one, covering her life from Belfast to Dohnavur. It is a mercy that she wrote about her experiences; but she never could have imagined that, one hundred years later, school-children in her own native land would study her life as a special project.

Just recently, I mentioned Amy and her work on Dr James Kennedy's *Coral Ridge Ministries* Television Programme in America, only to discover that Dr Kennedy had recently preached a public sermon about Amy! A few weeks ago, I was ministering God's Word at the *New Tribes Mission* European Headquarters at North Cotes, Humberside, England. It is a former Royal Air Force missile-base, bought by the Mission to train young missionaries and to house a Bible School. As I entered the huge site, I saw a large dormitory with a sign over the door, *Amy Carmichael*!

Just the other day, I received a phone call from the gifted evangelist, Roger Carswell, who told me that he had met an older lady in India, called Selva. Her father had been in prison for murder, and had come under the influence of Amy Carmichael. He became a Christian, and asked Amy to look after his children. He went to the gallows, singing a hymn. Roger then sent me a copy of a letter from Amy to Selva, that now lies on my desk. From 1919 onwards,

Amy wrote hundreds of letters to individual members of the Dohnavur family, or to groups. She was determined that nobody should be overlooked. She kept them all in a box, which was not to be opened until after her death. I take it that this is one of them. The letter speaks of how great a comfort Selva has been, and encourages her to continue to live to please the Lord Jesus. Amy tells Selva that if the letter ever gets into her hands, she should (by then) have seen her father, and "told him about you, and he will be glad."

The story of Amy Carmichael runs on and on! As I once heard my friend, Dr Raymond Brown, explain, heroes of the faith are no longer in the past: they are not history, they are in the future. They are part of the *cloud of witnesses* that have gone before us, urging us forward in the Christian battle.

In all, Amy wrote between thirty-five and forty books; depending on whether you count those which appeared in different forms. How could one sum up her style of writing in a word or two? I'd say it was 'awesome poetic-prose, mixed with blood and iron'. After all, what is art? "Art," said Count Leo Tolstoy, "is a human activity consisting in this, that one man consciously by means of certain external signs, hands on to others feelings he has lived through and that others are infected by these feelings and also experience them." [4] Well (apart from his male bias!), Tolstoy is right; and to read Amy Carmichael is to experience her strong, deep feelings, and to be infected by them. Generations of people have now shared in her feelings, and their influence ultimately points to the Christ whom she loved and served. One simply cannot miss Him at the heart of all she said and did.

As the years passed, another World War loomed; and Amy was to live through it, as she had the first one. As the world began to go on fire, one of Amy's dearest colleagues, Arulai, went to be with Christ. Soon after Amy's fall, Arulai caught smallpox. She never recovered completely. By 1939, Arulai was so weak that she was confined to bed in a room within sight of Amy's. They would exchange notes of prayer items and Bible verses. Arulai died on May 24th 1939, and Amy called it her Celestial Birthday. Amy once said that Arulai was "perhaps the most precious thing I have on earth." She had seen her as the future leader on the women's side of *The Dohnavur Fellowship* Ministry. But it was not to be. Amy faced her death, using the truth of what she called the *Trust of the Unexplained*. Amy had to learn to do without her.

In 1942, a Japanese invasion from Singapore was expected, and measures were taken. A plan for evacuation was drawn up, and supplies were quietly sent on up to the Forest. Fortunately, the invasion did not happen. Amy was not a pacifist, and a fair number of Dohnavur boys joined the Indian Army and Navy. During the Second World War the price of flour increased nine times. When it began, the needs at Dohnavur had cost £200 a year; now they cost upwards of £700 a week. Again, all their needs were supplied.

In 1946, Murray Webb-Peploe felt that he must go home to England to his wife and twin boys; and there is no doubt that his going gave Amy great pain. She felt his loss deeply, and stated, "No one is irreplaceable, so some say. That is a shallow lie." She urged the Fellowship to stand on the promise of Hebrews 13:5: . . . *I will never leave thee, nor forsake thee.*

Amy was now in her eightieth year. On June 23rd 1948, she fell in her bathroom and fractured the neck of her femur. In due course, a blood transfusion was started, but she reacted badly and it had to be stopped. Initially her pain was relieved by injections, and later by other measures. Trained nurses cared for her day and night.

Just before Christmas 1948, Godfrey Webb-Peploe had a thrombosis, and on February 19th 1949 he too went to be with Christ. The 'old guard' was passing on; and the very next day Amy wrote a letter to the Fellowship, finding it hard to separate the two brothers in her appreciation:

"I cannot tell what these two brothers have been to this Fellowship and Family, and to very many men and women, scattered about South India, their names are known and loved. I used to say to the Lord, 'Lord, if Thou dost give these brothers to be leaders of the Fellowship, it does not matter what happens to me. Let me be broken if only they may be strong and fit.' They have both gone and I am left quite broken, but content, for I know that we are safe in the hand of the Mighty and Loving One to whom this Fellowship belongs."

On the national scene, on Sunday 25th January 1948, the father of modern India, Mahatma Gandhi, who was two years younger than Amy, was viciously assassinated by Nathuram Vinayak Godse, as he hurried to a prayer ground for the regular evening devotions. He died murmuring, "Oh, God." It is fascinating to know that Gandhi's favourite Christian hymn was *When I survey the wondrous cross*.[5] A million and a half people marched after Gandhi's cortège to the Jumna River, and another million watched. Three aircraft showered countless rose petals on the procession. A million people were waiting at the cremation ground, and the pyre burned for fourteen hours. Requests for some of Gandhi's ashes came from all six continents, but they were denied. Fourteen days after his death, most of his remains were immersed in the rivers of India, according to Hindu ritual. His abiding memory on the world stage is his incredible lack of hatred and malice.

Interestingly, in 1939, back in Belfast at *The Welcome* Mission founded by Amy, a disciple of Gandhi, who had toured India with him, arrived to lead an Evangelistic Mission. Rev. Gnanai Jos, who had become a Christian, " . . . came to *The Welcome*, in the fullness of God," writes Pastor Edward Young. "The place was packed from the first night; many were standing outside the doors and windows trying to see and hear what was going on. One evening prior to his message, he gave out a hymn, *Who is on the Lord's side, Who will serve the King?* He got no further. A tall man, about six feet, stood up, saying, 'I will be on the Lord's side, I will serve the King.' No sooner had he said that, than many others in the congregation stood to their feet owning their allegiance to God. The Spirit of God swept through the hall. The preaching was set aside in order that souls could be dealt with. All over the church people were crying out for forgiveness and sanctification. What a mission that was. Many were the transactions made in Heaven during those days. Revival fires had been lit which continue to this day in many parts of the world."[6]

The 'father of modern India' had gone; and the mother of Dohnavur was going. Her very last *Dust of Gold* letter caught her mood: "If this letter reaches one who is cast down because of some failure or collapse, let these words be comfort, we have proved them true:

> Shepherd of Israel, what can baffle Love?
> Or cause Divine Compassion to remove?
> Out of a fall, Love makes a stepping-stone
> And quite reverses all the foe has done.
>
> Love, only love, these mighty things can do;
> What Love has purposed, love shall carry through.
> Oh, Love eternal, infinite, adored,
> I, even I, will sing unto the Lord.

'But'

19   IT WAS 1951. Colour television was introduced into
      the United States, and the first twenty-five U.S.
      Airforce F-86 Sabre Jets arrived in the United
Kingdom. Juan Fangio, the Argentinean racing driver, won the
European Grand Prix. The Festival of Britain was hugely popular
on the South Bank of the Thames, and the Oxford boat sank in the
annual boat race. It was reported that the average British housewife
worked a fifteen-hour day. Churchill was returned as Prime Minister;
Alvar Liddell and Robert Dougall were announced as BBC
Newsreaders.

The first hydrogen bomb was tested at Eniwetok Atoll in the
mid-Pacific; and electric power was produced by atomic energy for
the first time at Akron, Ohio. A joint Chinese and North Korean
offensive was launched on the Korean peninsula, and the city of
Seoul was taken. The British diplomats Burgess and Maclean, who
were in fact spies, escaped to the USSR. President Truman sacked
General MacArthur; and the U.S. Congress passed the 22nd
Amendment to the U.S. Constitution, ruling a maximum of two terms
of four years each for a U.S. president. The Shah of Persia married
his new wife, Soraya Esfandiary, whose wedding dress was
encrusted with $1.5 million worth of diamonds. Japan signed a peace
pact in San Francisco.

In London, R. Vaughan Williams' opera *The Pilgrim's Progress* was performed; but at Dohnavur, Amy Carmichael underlined a word in her copy of Bunyan's great work. It was the word *but*. Amy herself was beginning to approach the Celestial City. The word optimises her attitude to her own death. It is to be found in an extract concerning Christiana, Christian's wife: "At her departure her children wept. BUT Mr. Great-Heart and Mr. Valiant played upon the well-tuned cymbal and harp for joy."

Amy lived for two years and eight months following her fall on June 23rd 1948. Eventually, movement became virtually impossible, though as long as she could write, she did; and, when she could no longer join finger and thumb, she dictated. In 1949, a new milestone was reached for *The Dohnavur Fellowship*. Under the new system of Indian Government education, it was necessary to send some boys and girls to outside schools, in order that they might get the Leaving Certificate, necessary for almost any kind of training recognised by the Government.

Margaret Wilkinson, who is now retired and living in Castlerock, Co. Londonderry, persuaded Amy to allow the Dohnavur girls to join the Girl Guide Movement, and eventually a Girl Guide Company was formed. Margaret became an important bridge of communication with Amy to help the ministry at Dohnavur to move forward; and Amy began to accept other new proposals for *The Dohnavur Fellowship* work.

Slowly her journey on earth was coming to a close. Dr. Nancy Robbins is on record as testifying to an interesting conversation she had with Amy a few years before her fall of 1948. Amy had insisted that a certain lady also be allowed to help nurse her, who, in fact, did not provide adequate care. Dr. Robbins suggested that somebody more effective could be brought in. "Well," replied Amy, "nobody wants her, and I hope that I can help her." Shades of that old lady, coming down a Belfast street with her bundle, were still in Amy Carmichael's heart, as she turned in her own pain and weakness to help yet another person that nobody seemed to want. Now, though, Amy had trained help day and night.

By Christmas 1950, there were signs that the star that was Amy Carmichael was about to move on, to shine in another place. January 13th 1951 was the 59th Anniversary of her call on that memorable snowy evening at *Broughton Grange* in Cumbria. Amy began to sleep a lot, and the Dohnavur family was allowed to come in groups, and quietly enter her room to see her. Thankfully, her pain was gone, and a great quietness and stillness pervaded the *Room of Peace*. It is attested that even the birds in her aviary were silent. Amy slipped into a coma, and soon those around her could see that death was imminent – perhaps within an hour or two. Dr. Robbins tells that quite a number of the people to whom Amy was very close were called. Back in 1938, Amy believed that the Lord had promised to take her while she slept. And that is how she died, early on the morning of January 18th 1951, with her loved ones around her. Exactly according to Amy's wish, the bells in the Dohnavur House of Prayer played the music of one of her songs, based on the words of Psalm 27: 4: *One thing I have desired of the Lord, that will I seek after: that I may dwell in the house of the Lord all the days of my life, to behold the beauty of the Lord, and to inquire in His temple.* The words of Amy's song capture perfectly her deepest desire, which was to be at Home with Christ, which is 'far better'.

One thing have I desired, my God, of Thee,
That will I seek: Thy house be home to me.

I would not breathe an alien, other air;
I would be with Thee, O Thou fairest Fair.

For I would see the beauty of my Lord,
And hear Him speak, who is my heart's Adored.

O Love of loves, and can such wonder dwell
In Thy great Name of names – Immanuel?

Thou with Thy child; Thy child at home with Thee –
O Love of loves, I love, I worship Thee.

Great sadness descended on Dohnavur; but much joy also overflowed, as a result of the faithful Christian life of Amy Carmichael.

For a time Amy's body lay in a room, and soon her bed was completely covered with flowers that the children had brought for her. What pain she had spared them! What ultimate degradation and abuse! What life-long misery! Just like the Good Shepherd whom she followed, she had faced the wolf that would have taken the lambs; and though many times he tried to have her as well, she was victorious in the end, through the Lord's strength.

At noon, Amy's body was carried to the Dohnavur church in Dohnavur village: the boys and men lining up to form a bodyguard, older servants being her bearers. As the procession moved to the church, the boys sang a Tamil hymn; and in the church the boys continued to sing for an hour and a half, as both the Christian and Hindu community streamed in to pay Amy their last respects. The Bishop of Tirunelveli, G. T. Selwyn, a very close and longstanding friend of Amy's, led the service with others taking part, including two Indian men who paid tribute to her and to her work.

Amy's body was carried to the House of Prayer, and the tower bells rang out the tune of the hymn *Ten thousand times ten thousand*. Another special service was held there, and the congregation of men, women, schoolboys and girls, sang the words *Alleluia! The strife is o'er, the battle won*. A long stream of people, mostly dressed in white, and including children, moved out to God's Garden in the Dohnavur compound, where they waved ferns as a sign of victory.

At Amy's graveside, Devabakti read 1 Corinthians 15:50-58; and, when Amy had been laid to rest, the boys led the way around the garden which everyone encircled, coming back to the old tamarind tree at the entrance, pausing there for the end of the service. Tara led the unaccompanied singing, helped by her younger sisters – that is, her sisters through membership of Amy's 'family'. And there stood Preena. Fifty years before, as a seven year old child, she had arrived on Amy's verandah at around 6.30 a.m., as Amy was having her morning *chota*. She had escaped the Temple, where her little hands had been branded with hot irons; and the first thing Amy did was to lift her on to her lap and kiss her. She was the first of the temple children, who were to become Amy Carmichael's life-work. Preena's beloved *Ammai* (true mother) was now beholding the face of the One whose love had first constrained her to lay down her life for the gospel's sake.

And what now of Dohnavur? In 1989, a wish of Amy's was granted: the leadership of the work at Dohnavur passed into Indian hands. In 2001, the President of *The Dohnavur Fellowship*, Miss Sura Carunia, explained that the ties of family at Dohnavur are still very strong. Seven to eight children are still placed in 'cottage families', that are, of course, part of the bigger family. They are taught in school to Standard 5 in the Dohnavur Compound. Once this Elementary school period is completed, the ten–eleven year olds go to one of five different Christian Boarding Schools around the district. There is still plenty of fun and games; and many of the games still being played today were created by Amy. Through Amy's love of nature, trees, flowers, plants, birds and animals were represented in a song, which was made into a game. Songs are called 'wings', because of their uplifting power.

All kinds of activities continue at Dohnavur. The elderly make gifts for the patients at the hospital, and some also make toys. Some script beautiful texts of Scripture on to wood. In the hospital there is a pathological laboratory, an extensive pharmacy, an operating theatre, and even dental services. Three doctors see three–four hundred patients per day. Now computers handle office administration – Amy's website would surely have been worth reading!

Boys are no longer received by *The Dohnavur Fellowship*, due to the fact that none was coming; and, in any case, there were no men available to look after them. But, on the campus of what was once the Dohnavur Home for Boys, a wonderful new Boarding School is now at full vigour. It provides Christian education and home care for over five hundred and seventy children between the ages of five and seventeen. Their parents are working in many parts of India with a number of different Missions and organisations, especially in remote areas with the underprivileged. It is called Santhosha

Vidhyalaya, meaning 'Happy Place of Knowledge'. The Principal, Mr. Ponraj, explains that each Indian State is like a different country in the European Community, with a different culture, language, food, set of habits, and clothing. When missionaries move from one State to another, it is very difficult to have their children educated; so the necessity for the Boarding School at Dohnavur became apparent. Currently, children representing twenty-six of the thirty-two States of India, speaking thirteen different languages, attend the school.

Only girls are taken by *The Dohnavur Fellowship*. If not received, many would become victims of infanticide, a practice that is sadly widespread as a way of coping with poverty and unwanted female babies. This problem stems particularly from the huge cost of weddings in India. As dowries are very expensive, sadly some mothers will kill or abandon an unwanted daughter. (Let us not forget, though, that in the so-called civilised West infanticide also takes place on a very large scale; albeit some months earlier.) The home at *Three Pavilions* looks after girls who are physically or mentally disabled, and the Centre by the sea at Joppa still brings deep refreshment.

On Amy's birthday, every December 16th, the entire family of *The Dohnavur Fellowship* meets at Dohnavur for a grand feast. Few of them will ever visit the little village of Millisle in Co. Down, where Amy Beatrice Carmichael was born on December 16th 1867. The oyster-catchers and curlews, redshanks and ringed plovers, Icelandic gulls, cormorants and Brent geese still fly to the County Down coast. Quite recently, I watched my twin daughters, Kerrie and Claire, being baptised by immersion in the Millisle Lagoon, yards from the front door of Amy Carmichael's maternal home. As their church family gathered around them, and sang praises to the Lord near those pools that Amy had played in, their praise certainly took wings. It was all very uplifting, and their father was thinking long, long thoughts.

In *Though the Mountains Shake*, published in 1943, Amy wrote what she felt Dohnavur would look like to a wild bird:

"A bird flying overhead would see the Place of our Beginning, rather like a slice of forest which had slipped down from the Western hills and settled on the Plains. For we have many trees. The bird would see small red roofs nestling low, and here and there a taller one pushing up through the green. But the bird would not mind how many roofs there were, for all the land within our gates is sanctuary to birds."

It is hauntingly fitting that the memorial at the Wild-bird child's grave in God's Garden at Dohnavur is a birdbath. It reads, simply, *Ammai*.

The Law Of Liberty

20　IT WAS 2003. The coalition war in Iraq brought down the regime of Saddam Hussein. In Africa, the epidemic of AIDS reached mammoth proportions, and it was shown that time was running out. Without a campaign to make treatment available to all, it was predicted that 5-6 million South Africans alone would die of AIDS by 2010. In the Middle East, the dispute between the Israelis and Palestinians continued to take many lives. A draft of United Europe's first Constitution was presented. The infamous 'green line' dividing Cyprus began finally to break down.

In the United States, Gregory Peck died. He was the actor who got the role of the heroic Atticus Finch in the film of Harper Lee's Pulitzer-prize-winning novel, *To Kill a Mockingbird*. Lee kindly and truly said that Peck played himself. In England, Sir J. Paul Getty Jr. died, having given more than two hundred million dollars to charity. Lord Archer got out of jail; and Tanya Streeter created history, when she held her breath for three minutes and thirty-nine seconds after descending four hundred feet into the ocean, and resurfacing by her own power. In *The Times* of July 22nd Dr. Thomas Stuttaford stated: "I am not certain that reducing the lungs to the size of an orange, even if they are lungs that have been accustomed to deep diving, is a desirable aim. Now that Streeter has achieved the world record, it might be the time to retire from the competition and develop an interest in shell collecting or bird watching."

In the month of June 2003, I found myself speaking to several Primary School classes at Harmony Hill Primary School in the City of Lisburn, at the request of a schoolteacher called Mrs. Ruth Baillie. She had heard that I was writing about the Wild-bird child, and as the children in the school had been studying Amy's life she wondered if I might talk to them about her. What a morning I had! When I had traced Amy's life with the children, I opened the session for questions, and they 'rained' on me. I then set a competition, asking the children to write an essay on what had impressed them about Amy's life. Their response was remarkable. "The thing that I liked about Amy was that whether you were rich or poor, old or young, boy or girl, she was always willing to help you," wrote Rebecca. Emma was impressed with the fact that Amy "never gave up on God, and was able to love all those children and raise them without giving up." To Simon, it was the fact that "Whenever she prayed to God, God answered her prayers." Apart from other things she listed, Natasha was touched by the way the children of Dohnavur laid flowers on Amy's bed in death; and "when it was time to have the funeral, they did their best to have the best one for the one they called Amma." Laura was moved by the fact that, "even though she was an invalid, Amy still helped India." Many more fascinating impressions were presented to me.

When I asked the children to guess what marked Amy's grave, I had eventually to stop their enthusiastic and tastefully imaginative suggestions! To me, the Wild-bird child's bird bath seemed to be an iconic climax to that truly memorable morning!

As I close this book, I want to soar in my imagination away from those enthusiastic children, still able to be inspired by the life of Amy Carmichael in the twenty-first century, to Holy Trinity Church on the north side of Clapham Common near London, in the eighteenth century.

Amongst its parishioners was one of the most influential groups of Christians who ever lived. There you would have found Zachary Macaulay, one of the first Governors of Sierra Leone and the father of the great Victorian historian. Sickened by the slave trade, Zachary became an expert on the subject, and was resolved to stamp it out. He was supported in this by another parishioner at Holy Trinity, Henry Thornton. Thornton was a banker, a Member of Parliament, and the principal backer of the Sierra Leone Company set up to repatriate former slaves then living in London. There, too, you would have found one of the great giants of the Christian faith, the Christian orator, politician, and slave emancipator, William Wilberforce.

At Wilberforce's Queen Anne house, with its beautiful, oval-shaped library, some truly distinguished people would gather: diplomats, legislators, businessmen, and Members of Parliament, all committed to the abolition of the slave trade. There, too, you would have found the Rector of Holy Trinity, Rev. John Venn. In history, they have been nicknamed 'The Clapham Saints' and 'The Clapham Sect'. "I look on them as a group of pools, which I am seeking to make into a river against slavery," said Wilberforce.

In fact, it became a mighty river that extended a long way beyond Clapham. It brought with it Wilberforce's friend, Prime Minister William Pitt, the Younger – at twenty-four years of age, the youngest Prime Minister in British history. It also brought with it the ex-slaver John Newton, who wrote the hymn *Amazing Grace*; Edmund Burke; John Wesley; the poet, Samuel Taylor Coleridge; and the great pottery manufacturer, Josiah Wedgwood. Tens of thousands of the public eventually signed protests against slavery. Wilberforce was an active participant in sixty-nine different public initiatives, ranging from founding the world's first Bible Society, and helping to found the Sierra Leone colony for freed slaves; to the Royal Society for the Prevention of Cruelty to Animals, the Royal Institute of Science, and the National Gallery. His crowning achievements were the abolition of the slave trade in 1807, and the abolition of slavery in the British Empire in 1833.

On July 26th 1833, the final passage of the Emancipation Bill was ensured, when a committee of the House of Commons worked out the key details. Three days later, Wilberforce died. For fifty years, his book *A Practical View of Christianity* was a best seller. The historian, G. M. Trevelyan, described abolition as "one of the turning points in the history of the world." As Count Pecchio wrote, "When Mr.

Wilberforce passes through a crowd on the day of the Opening of Parliament, every one contemplates this little old man, worn with age, his head sunk upon his shoulders, as a sacred relic; as the Washington of humanity."

Although Wilberforce is remembered primarily for his work with his friends in abolishing the slave trade, I want to highlight another incredibly important initiative that he took, as led by the hand of God. From the group at Clapham there also stirred an interest in Christian mission that was part of a movement of the Spirit of God with a new, not-for-profit, rationale. As Professor Niall Ferguson states in his book *Empire*, "It was to be the defining mission of the century's most successful non-governmental organisations (NGO's)."[1] Famous missionary societies were formed, like the London Missionary Society, which sent Livingstone to Africa. This has resulted in the conversion of millions to Christ, so that now the African Continent is more Christian than Europe. Let it never be forgotten that Livingstone did not go to Africa with some haughty, cultural chauvinism that dismissed African society. He once wrote that he did not believe "in any incapacity of the African, in either mind or heart. . . . In reference to the status of Africans among the nations of the earth, we have seen nothing to justify the notion that they are of a different 'breed' or 'species' from the most civilised."[2]

The Baptists' great missionary society was founded by the Godly William Carey; and the Anglicans established the Church Missionary Society; so that there are now, for example, more Anglicans in Nigeria than in England. Scottish societies were formed in Glasgow and Edinburgh; and there was, of course, the society through which Amy Carmichael entered India, the Church of England Zenana Missionary Society.

Until the early nineteenth century, the British in India had not the slightest interest in missionary activity. The East India Company, a privately-owned stock company, had done business in India on behalf of Britain since 1613; but its chaplains were explicitly banned from preaching to the Indians themselves. The company used its power to restrict the entry of missionaries into India. William Carey, for example, was forced to reside in the Danish enclave of Serampore, along with all other Christian missionaries who wished to work in India.

This all changed, with the 'river' from Clapham. Charles Grant (1746-1823), who had risen to a place of prominence in India while working for the East India Company, became a believer after he lost two children to smallpox. He rose to become a Chairman and Director of the East India Company, and a Member of Parliament. He was deeply dismayed by some cruel customs he found in India, and by the immorality and indifference of British rulers of the country. He believed that missionaries could help, and he found allies in the group at Clapham. In 1813, the East India Company's charter came due for renewal. The group at Clapham mobilised public opinion, petitioning half-a-million signatures.

On the night of June 22nd 1813, Wilberforce rose to address a full House of Commons. He spoke for three hours, and virtually turned the place into a church service. It is said that he simply enraptured his audience. He had done his 'homework'; and this, combined with the fire of his deep evangelical faith and the glowing language of his heart, had his listeners enthralled. He spoke against the condescending nature of the caste system, and showed how the message of the gospel succoured the needy, comforted the sorrowful, and visited the forsaken. Implacably opposed to the practice of *suttee* (the former Hindu practice of a widow taking her life by throwing herself on her husband's funeral pyre – the only 'religious practice' legislated against by the British Raj) and other cruelties, the great slave emancipator rebutted the charge that he was advocating compulsory conversion to Christianity. "Compulsion and Christianity!" he cried. "Why, the very terms are at variance with each other – the ideas are incompatible. In the language of inspiration itself, Christianity has been called 'the law of liberty.'" He was not asking, he said, for Parliament to organise or ordain evangelism; he was asking, "that we should not substantially, and in effect, prevent others from engaging in it."

Incredibly, both the House of Commons and the House of Lords responded positively to Wilberforce's plea; and the subsequent East India Company Charter of 1883 gained a 'Missionary clause'. This guaranteed complete liberty to the propagation of the Christian faith in India. The slave emancipator from Hull had put the key in a firmly locked door, that led eventually to the legendary work of Amy Carmichael and her colleagues freeing children from things that 'darkened the sun'.

On March 25th 1784, the diarist James Boswell and his friend Samuel Johnston heard the young Wilberforce speak at a political meeting in York. More than four thousand people were present as they saw Wilberforce mount a table to address the crowd. Boswell said later that he had seen a little fellow on a table speaking, and described him as 'a perfect shrimp'. "But presently," he added, "the shrimp swelled into a whale." When the 'whale' surfaced in the Palace of Westminster in 1813, those who saw him watched in awe. The waves from that surfacing are still affecting the history of Christian missions.

So it was that, in the fullness of time, Amy Carmichael not only became an outstanding Christian missionary, but her Christian faith led her to become a compassionate and articulate social reformer in direct line to the gifted Evangelicals of the early eighteenth century. Like those Evangelicals before her, did Amy insist that salvation can be found only and in none other than Christ; and that there is *no other name under heaven given among men, whereby we must be saved*? She most certainly did. Did she believe that Jesus is God incarnate; that He arose bodily from the grave, ascended into heaven, and that He is literally coming back again? She believed these things with a deep passion. Did she always practise her Christian faith without fault? She would have been the first to say that she did not. Did she make mistakes? Of course she did. Yet, in her lifetime of commitment to the gospel of Jesus Christ, by the grace of God she often mirrored the greatest of all Christian missionaries, Paul the Apostle. Please note, this statement is not an exaggeration by an uncritical biographer. A short study of the parallels will suffice.

Amy did not rob temples, or blaspheme their gods (see Acts 19:37). She did not make money out of religion (see Acts 20:33-35). She was no crude, political activist; nor, even in her dealings with outlaws, did she support terrorism (see Acts 21:37-39). She was no ignorant, uneducated, sectarian demagogue either (see Acts 22:3). Thomas Walker gave her a very strict education in the Tamil language, and instilled in her a deep respect for it. Amy was no 'Raj' establishment figure; her deepest wish

was that Indians should one day lead her work – and her wish has been fulfilled. Amy also worked widely across the Christian community. It is also important to note that the books in Amy's library, which were a deep source of her intellectual life, prove that she respected the good in the writings of others who would have differed with her on many issues.

Amy did not do her awesome work in a corner, that's for sure (see Acts 26:24-26). What she unearthed of an outrageous practice was submitted to the highest authorities of her day; and was subsequently seen for what it was by the Indian authorities who banned it. Like Paul, Amy believed that what Moses and the prophets said would happen, did happen; namely, that Christ would suffer, be the first to rise from the dead, and would proclaim light to His own people and to the Gentiles (see Acts 26:22-23). She sincerely believed that she had been commanded to carry that light to others. The Hindu and Christian people, who flocked into the church at Dohnavur to pay their respects at her death, proved that she had carried that light with great sensitivity, dignity and grace. On a world-wide scale, subsequent generations continue to rise up and thank God for her life and memory.

At the close of this biography I should like to emphasise what I believe is a very important matter. While this book has necessarily dealt with a terrible evil, I would not want any reader to even suspect that this characterises the whole of India and all the Hindu population. I know how I would feel if a book was filled with the horrors and cruelties that have gone on in Northern Ireland, and presented it as a picture of the Province as a whole. It simply would not be true. Not all orthodox Hindus approved of what went on in some (not all) of their temples. It was, in fact, an Indian woman doctor who introduced a Bill in the Madras Legislative Assembly, prohibiting the dedication of little girls to the deities in Hindu temples. This Bill became law just one year after India's independence. A similar Bill was passed by a majority vote in the Central Government in Delhi in 1954. The fact that these measures were taken, first by a State Government, and then by the All India Parliament, speaks volumes for the concern there is in India about such practices.

In July 2003, the population of India was 1,049,700,118, 80% being Hindu. There are many Hindus who have high moral standards. For example, some were genuinely shocked when some years ago India was flooded with 'hippies' from the so-called 'Christian' West, who seemed curiously without any moral standards.

It also needs to be emphasised that, while Amy Carmichael was grieved and hurt by much nominal Christianity among missionaries and the Indian churches, it was not her intention to say that this represented all that went on. It is a pleasure to report that there are today many wonderful Indian missionaries who love their nation, and who are deeply devoted to the Lord Jesus Christ. These dedicated people are prepared to stand up and be counted, and to speak out against the evil in today's society. I want to send out a message of deep appreciation from Amy Carmichael's native land for all the great things that they are doing for their nation, and for the Christian cause.

In Amy's native land, I have recently been involved in speaking to hundreds of young people in many schools about their dreams for the future. I have been pleased to discover that significant numbers of these young people want to be involved in helping developing countries. This trend has been highlighted by Dr. Alan Gillespie CBE, former Chief Executive of the CDC – previously the Commonwealth Development Corporation; an Ulsterman himself. When delivering the 2003 inaugural City Lecture, on behalf of the

Judge Institute of Management at the University of Cambridge, and the Worshipful Company of Actuaries in London, he said:

"In particular I think of young people, those going on gap year assignments, or those going away after university. I find that today many do not want to go to the city law firms, or investment banks, but rather want to work in the business of development." He encouraged his audience to "become informed, critical and have well-worked ideas," on the topic of how to help developing countries. He advised them to "have a point of view, enter the development policy arguments, and become opinion leaders in this debate." He urged them to "recognise and support great causes, movements and policy mobilisations." Such would need "good advocacy, lobbying, professional support, and sensible guidance." He asked his audience to "engage with your institutional clientele-corporations, pension funds, insurance companies, trusts and foundations, to help them understand the value and appropriateness of some proportion of their capital being allocated to poorer countries, both as a moral duty and as a financial opportunity."

He told them to "become an encourager, an adviser to those who want to get involved." He saw a possible brighter scenario in the future: ". . . driven by private investment and widespread entrepreneurial activity. Under this scenario, the economies of developing countries grow vigorously, jobs are created, wealth is generated and hundreds of millions of new consumers come into the global market place each year. Nations such as China, India, South Africa and Brazil become major engines of economic growth and their prosperity infects their neighbours. This results in major decrease in global poverty; social well-being improves, civil society is stabilised and conflict is reduced. This is an era of innovation, competition and economic energy emanating from developing countries, enabling a step change in development. In this scenario, poverty, disease, illiteracy and want are seriously reduced. This is the outcome we are all looking for."

I also hear other voices calling for us in the West to get involved in the needs of developing countries. One of the most outstanding is that of the Christian, Baroness Cox – a deputy Speaker in the House of Lords. Like Wilberforce before her, she has become a voice for the voiceless. She has even purchased slaves, in order to expose the present day slave trade.

Of course, Dr Gillespie and Baroness Cox would be the first to remind me that *man shall not live by bread alone*. I am thrilled to report that recently, in Northern Ireland in particular, there has been a significant rise in hundreds of young people going across the world in their school holidays and gap years. Constrained by the love of Christ, they build houses, paint schools, help the victims of crime and drug abuse, give help to street children and the victims of AIDS, etc. As they travel and work, they are constantly spreading the news that Jesus Christ is the answer to the deepest needs of the hearts and lives of people in every corner of the earth. They are highlighting the fact that Christ is the Bread of Life, and can satisfy the spiritual hunger of every heart that turns to Him in repentance and faith. It is one of the most heartening things I have witnessed in my lifetime. I am convinced that more 'Wild-bird' children are on their way!

It was the great Social Reformer, Lord Shaftesbury, who once wrote that nobody can persist from the beginning of their life to the end of it in a course of generosity, or a course of virtue, unless they are "drawing from the fountain of our Lord Himself." In the light of that statement, and as I now lay down my pen on this life of Amy Carmichael, I want to ask, and answer, some questions:

> What inspired the daughter of Millisle,
> Who was in essence a *Wild-bird child*?
> Who led her to the hell-holes of evil, then?
> To face down the sickening power of sin?
> Who kept her sweet amidst what was sour,
> Who inched her step to scale Satan's tower?
> What caused her to dip her pen deep into ink,
> To influence millions to rethink
> The true purpose of life and the use of gift,
> And pure gold from much dross to sift?
> It was the Lord.

Who gave the light that in darkness shone,
That still reaches us when she is gone?
Who strengthened her mind, when many a tongue
Strove to silence the beautiful song she had sung?
Who guided her from Millisle to Bangalore,
And on to the confines of Dohnavur?
Who kept her, despite horrendous sorrow,
Feeding hungry mouths, and not having to borrow
A single, solitary, useful rupee?
Who raised her service to such a high degree?
It was the Lord.

Who led Preena out through that Temple door,
The first of many hundreds more?
Who protected Amy when, in disguise,
She discovered what caused those midnight cries?
Who led her on to the national scene,
To highlight a practice that should not have been?
Who helped her put Raj's story into prose,
Himsa's horrors to subtly expose?
Who raised that Forest House by waterfall and pool,
Where laughing, joyous children cooled?
It was the Lord.

Who gave the courage to endure
Illness, that appeared to have no cure?
Who gave her patience to accept
That, for year on year, she must be kept
Within the limits of the Room of Peace,
Which stretched into a twenty-one year lease?
Who guided her pen, in those years of pain,
To write thirteen books, which were to gain
Immeasurable influence across the earth,
Which showed no sign of creative dearth?
It was the Lord.

Can we all know, in the challenge of life,
In a new millennium of international strife,
The secret of the *Wild-bird child*,
In an age far removed from her lifestyle?
Can we mount up with wings as an eagle, too,
And constantly have our strength renewed?
Can we run and not be weary, then,
And walk and not faint, again and again?
The secret is simple, and for all to know;
And may our hearts in its knowledge grow:
It is the Lord.

Where, then, do I leave the Wild-bird child? She gave her formidable life to the rescue of children, and she firmly believed that there was a safe place, where they could live forever. I want to quote further from her poem *Lift up thy heart*. The following words are an exquisite expression of Amy Carmichael's view of Heaven. They are her invaluable legacy, her unique gift of words, to all those who have had their hearts broken through the bereavement of little children. In my honest opinion, they are the most moving words she ever penned.

O thou bereaved and not comforted,
Lift up thy heart, lift up thine eyes, and look
And see the things that are.
                    A singing land
Lies there above the clouds and the grey rain:
Sighing and tears have never found the way
That leads from earth to it – nor pain, nor sin;
Baffled, they fall back on the troubled world
And walk about down here. Dost thou love rivers?
A river flows through all that goodly land.
Dost love the sunshine and the shade of trees?
There is no night there; but lest any heat
Should hurt, the light comes filtered through the leaves

Of the immortal Tree. The flowers there,
Coloured with happiness, forget to fade;
Each fern uncurls in individual joy;
The very mosses and the lichens paint
The rocks with conscious pleasure; and the birds –
Oh, they are eagerer than even ours
To pour live joy into the air, an air
That seems alive, instinct with joy of life.
And the earth underfoot laughs softly, buds;
And the dear, shy buds smile.
                    The children, see,
Gayer at games they are than even here,
Keener at work; for, look, the Wonder Schools
Open their secrets to them, secrets shut
Fast from us mortals. And the men and maids
Do nobler deeds than ever they had dared
To dream in limited days; for never bar
Is set to high endeavour; but to think –
So pure their thoughts – is gloriously to do,
And with swift ease. For that city is not paved
With wasted powers; no lost or futile loves
Lie like fair fallen petals on the walks
Of its great gardens; else the word that calls
Him blessed whom God, choosing out, receives
And satisfies with the pleasure of His house,
Were dust and ashes. And it never was God's way
To feed the soul He made on vanity.

Therefore, I take it to be verity
That those things are, yea, tenfold better things,
And that our own enjoy them, they being still
Our own, not stranger folk of alien mind,
Removed, aloof. The love we knew is there,
The cheerfulness, the courage, faithfulness
To duty, and forgetfulness of self –

But perfected in holiness. And they,
Living their stainless lives in joyousness,
Are still themselves, and wait to hear thy step
(Their hearts will know it, though a thousand thronged
Together at the door); yet they, having seen
The end of the Lord, are well content to wait.

And the Wild-bird child, where is she? Let her own words tell us, from her poem *No wandering bird am I*:

Nearness to Thee, O God, is all my good;
No wandering bird am I in dark'ning wood.
In my tall Tree of Life my nest is set,
Sheltered by careful leaves from winds that fret.

No fowler climbs so high to fling his snare;
No prowling thing of night can breathe that air.
Under Thy covering wings Thy bird would dwell;
Safe nested in my Tree, all, all is well.

BIBLIOGRAPHY

This list is intended to indicate the principal works from which I have drawn in my research, to acknowledge my debt to their authors, as well as to provide some suggestions for further reading.

Boreham, F. W., *A Handful of Stars,* The Epworth Press, 1933.

Dick, Lois Hoadley, *Amy Carmichael: Let the Little Children Come*, Moody Press, Chicago, 1984.

Elliot, Elizabeth, *A Chance To Die: The Life and Legacy of Amy Carmichael*, Fleming H. Revell : A Division of Baker Book House Co. Grand Rapids, Michigan 49516, 2002.

Ferguson, Niall, *Empire,* Allen Lane, The Penguin Press, 2003.

Fischer, Louis, *The Life of Mahatma Gandhi*, Harper Collins, 1997.

Grun, Bernard, *The Timetables of History, The New Third Revised Edition*, Simon and Schuster/Touchstone, 1991.

Guedalla, Philip, *Mr. Churchill, A Portrait*, Hodder and Stoughton Limited, 1943.

Hancock, Christopher D., *William Wilberforce,* Christian History, <u>Christianity Today</u>, 465 Gundersen Drive, Carol Sheen, Il.60188, U.S.A., Winter 1997.

Hough, Richard, *Edwina, Countess Mountbatten of Burma,* Sphere Books Limited, 1985.

Legrand, Jacques, *Chronicle of the 20th century* , JL International Publications, 1993.

Manchester, William, *The Last Lion, Winston Spencer Churchill; Visions of Glory 1874-1932,* Sphere Books Limited, 1984 .

Pollock, John, *Wilberforce,* Lion Publishing plc, 1986.

Williams, Derek, *The Spirit of Keswick,* Keswick Convention Trust, 1988.

Young, Edward, *That In All Things He might Have The Pre-Eminence: A Short History of the First 100 Years of the Welcome Evangelical Church,* 1987. Published by Welcome Evangelical Church.

David Abram, Devdan Sen, Nick Edwards, Beth Woolbridge and Mike Ford, *South India, The Rough Guide, The Rough Guides Ltd., London, 1999.*

ENDNOTES

Preface

1.	Quoted on the back page of the 1979 Edition of E. M. Forster's *A Passage to India*, Penguin Books, 1979.

2.	Quoted with the permission of Dr. Os Guinness.

Chapter 1

1.	Source for this story is found in *A Handful of Stars* by F. W. Boreham, The Epworth Press, 1933, pp.178-180.

Chapter 3

1.	Source for this story is *The Spirit of Keswick* by Derek Williams, Keswick Convention Trust, 1988, pp.11, 12.

2.	*Victoria College, Belfast*, Centenary Publication, 1959, p.15.

3.	David Abram, Devdan Sen, Nick Edwards, Beth Woolbridge and Mike Ford, *South India, The Rough Guide,* The Rough Guides Ltd., London, 1999, Introduction, Xl.

Chapter 5

1.	Elizabeth Elliot, *A Chance to Die*, Fleming H. Revell: A Division of Baker Book House Co., Grand Rapids, Michigan 49516, 2002, p.287.

Chapter 6

1. Author's explanation of the Betel Nut in Asian culture.

Chapter 7

1- 3 Louis Fischer, *The Life of Mahatma Ghandi,* Harper Collins, 1997, pp.214, 19, 20.

4-7 Quoted by Louis Fischer, as above, pp.21, 22.

8-12 Quoted by William Manchester in *The Last Lion, Winston Spencer Churchill; Visions of Glory 1874-1932*, Sphere Books Ltd., 1984, pp.202-205.

Chapter 8

1. Rudyard Kipling, *The Works of Rudyard Kipling,* Wordsworth Poetry Library, Wordsworth Editions Ltd., 1994, p.329.

2. Quoted by Niall Ferguson, *Empire,* Allen Lane, The Penguin Press, 2003, p.181.

Chapter 10

1-2 Quoted by Lois Hoadley Dick in *Amy Carmichael: Let The Little Children Come,* Moody Press, 1984, p.36.

Chapter 15

1. A book written by Amy.

Chapter 17

1. Quoted by Elizabeth Elliot in *A Chance to Die,* Fleming H. Revell: A Division of Baker Book House Co., Grand Rapids, Michigan, 49516, 2002, p.291.

Chapter 18

1. Quoted by Richard Hough in *Edwina, Countess Mountbatten of Burma,* Sphere Books Limited, 1985, p.195.

2. Quoted by Richard Hough, as above, p.199.

3. Quoted in *Amy Carmichael*, An Inter-Board Religious Education Project For Key Stage Two R. E., undated, p.4.

4. Count Leo Tolstoy, *What is Art?* 1898.

5. Edward Young, *That In All Things He Might Have The Pre-Eminence: A Short History of The First 100 Years of the Welcome Evangelical Church,* published by The Welcome Evangelical Church, 1987, p.15.

6. Louis Fischer, *The Life of Mahatma Gandhi,* Harper Collins, 1997, p.284.

Chapter 20

1. Niall Ferguson, *Empire*, Allen Lane, The Penguin Press, 2003, p.123.

2. Quoted by Niall Ferguson in the above, p.133.

3. Quoted by John Pollock, *Wilberforce*, Lion Publishing plc, 1986, p.238.

4. This challenging and thoughtful speech is quoted with the kind permission of Dr. Alan Gillespie, CBE.

Amy Carmichael's Published Works

1895	From Sunrise Land	London: Marshall Brothers
1901	From the Fight	London: CEZMS/Marshall Brothers
1901	Raisins and God's Missionary (= God's Missionary)	Madras: SPCK
1903	Things as they Are (Mission-work in S. India)	London: Morgan & Scott
1906	Overweights of Joy	London: Morgan & Scott
1908	Beginning of a Story	London: Morgan & Scott
1909	Lotus Buds	Madras: SPCK
1914	Continuation of a Story	London: Morgan & Scott
1916	Walker of Tirunelveli	London: Morgan & Scott
1917	Made in the Pans	London/Edinburgh: Oliphants Ltd.
1918	Ponnammal: Her Story	London: Morgan & Scott
1920	From the Forest	London/Edinburgh: Oliphants Ltd.
1921	Dohnavur Songs	Madras: SPCK
1922	Nor Scrip	Madras: SPCK/Marshall Brothers UK
1923	Ragland, Pioneer	Madras: SPCK
1924	Tables in the Wilderness	Madras: SPCK
1924	The Valley of Vision	
1924,5,6,30	Mimosa	London: SPCK
1926	Raj, Brigand Chief	London: Seeley, Service & Co.
1928	The Widow of the Jewels	London: SPCK
1929	Meal in a Barrel	Madras: CLS
1932	Gold Cord	London: SPCK
1933	Rose from Brier	London: SPCK
1934	Ploughed Under	London: SPCK
1935	Gold by Moonlight	London: SPCK
1936	Toward Jerusalem	London: SPCK
1937	Windows	London: SPCK
1938	If	London: SPCK
1938	Figures of the True	London: SPCK
1938	Pools and the Valley of Vision	London: SPCK

1939	Kohila, The Shaping of an Indian Nurse	London: SPCK
1939	God's Missionary	London: SPCK
1941	His Thoughts Said . . . His Father Said	London: SPCK
1943	Though the Mountains Shake	London: SPCK
1948	Before the Door Shuts	Madras: Diocesan Press
1950	This One Thing – The Story of Walker of Tirunelveli	London/Edinburgh: Oliphants Ltd.
1955	Edges of His Ways – Daily Readings	London: SPCK
1958	Thou Givest . . . They Gather	London: Lutterworth
1959	Wings Part 1 (Songs)	London: SPCK
1981	Candles in the Dark	London: SPCK
1982	Whispers of His Power	London: SPCK Triangle/ New York: Fleming Revell
1987	Fragments that Remain	London: SPCK Triangle
2001	Kohila (colour-illustrated reprint)	Dohnavur Fellowship

<u>Note</u>: SPCK no longer publish any of Amy's books. CLC has taken over a number of them (see list).

Books of Amy Carmichael currently published by CLC, P.O. Box 1449, Fort Washington, Pennsylvania, 19034, United States of America

Candles in the Dark
Edges of His Ways
Figures of the True
God's Missionary
Gold by Moonlight

Gold Cord
His Thoughts Said . . . His Father Said
If
Kohila (published by *Dohnavur* in India)
Mimosa
Mountain Breezes (Collection 566 of Amy's poems)
Rose from Brier
Thou Givest . . . They Gather
Toward Jerusalem

See also:

Blanch, Stuart and Brenda,	*Learning from God,* (an anthology from Amy Carmichael's works)	CLC
Robbins, Dr. Nancy,	*Patients and Patience*	*
Skoglund, Elizabeth,	*Amma,*	Baker Books, USA/Alpha Publishing, UK
Wilkinson, Margaret	*At BBC Corner* *I remember Amy Carmichael*	*

* Available from
The Dohnavur Fellowship,
UK Office,
15 Elm Drive,
Harrow,
Middlesex,
England
HA2 7BS
Website: www.dohnavurfellowship.org

CHRONOLOGY

1867	Amy is born in Millisle in beautiful County Down, Ireland, on December 16th.
1870	Amy prays the most famous prayer of her life, when she asks God for two blue eyes and learns that 'No' is an answer.
1879	Enters Marlborough House boarding school in Harrogate, after being educated by a succession of governesses. She is the eldest of seven children: Amy, Norman, Ernest, Eva, Ethel, Walter and Alfred.
Circa 1883	Amy is converted to Christ through the ministry of the Children's Special Service Mission in Harrogate.
1885	Amy's father, David Carmichael, dies of double pneumonia on April 12th at 54 years of age.
1887	Founds *The Welcome*, a ministry to linen mill girls from a hall on Cambrai Street in the Shankill area of Belfast.
Circa 1887	Becomes editor of a family magazine *Scraps*, which shows her early promise as a writer. In time the magazine is to become the vehicle for her future, historic letters.
1889	Begins work in the slums of Manchester with Manchester City Mission.
1890	Moves to Broughton Grange in Cumbria.
1891	Is called to overseas service one snowy evening in January.
1893-1894	Serves as a missionary in Japan.
1895	Serves for a short period in Ceylon.
1896	Begins her lifetime of service amongst the people of India.
1896-1898	Moves to work in the Tirunelveli District of South India with *The Starry Cluster*.
1899	Preena escapes to Amy; her entire ministry changes direction.

1900   Amy moves permanently to Dohnavur, and begins to save children from the Temples.

1902   Amy is a speaker at the annual Convention of the Reformed Syrian Church, attended by as many as 20,000 people.

1903   Amy publishes *Things As They Are* and causes a stir.

1905   Amy writes a letter saying that she hopes to gather facts concerning the Temple children, and then to approach the Government upon the subject.

1906   Lala dies, and there is an epidemic of cholera in village of Dohnavur.

1907   Mabel Wade arrives to help Amy, and the first gift is given to build nurseries.

1911   Amy faces the possibility of imprisonment because of Muttammal.

1912   Thomas Walker, Amy's teacher and mentor, dies.

1913   Mrs. Catherine Jane Carmichael, Amy's mother, dies in London.

1914   The Dohnavur family now numbers 130, and Kohila is rescued.

1915   Ponnammal dies.

1917   Grey Jungle land is purchased, and the wonderful Forest House is built. In the early days at the Grey Jungle, a child, while learning to swim, suddenly seizes Amy and drags her under water. Amy just escapes drowning.

1918   The first baby boy is accepted at Dohnavur, and the rescue work for boys begins. The First World War ends. During the war, incredible answers to prayer experienced at Dohnavur.

1919   Lord Pentland writes to Amy to inform her that she has been mentioned in the Birthday Honours List. She is given the Kaiser-i-Hind Medal for service to the people of India.

1921   On October 12th the 'Robin Hood' of South India and two of his men way-lay Amy in order to talk with her. It all leads to an unforgettable adventure.

1923   Twenty nurseries established at Dohnavur.

1924   Dr. May Powell arrives to work permanently at Dohnavur.

1926   Godfrey Webb-Peploe arrives to stay at Dohnavur, and eighty boys are rescued.

1927   £100 is given to begin building a hospital, and the beautiful House of Prayer is built.

1928   Dr. Murray Webb-Peploe arrives to stay, and land is purchased for the boys work.

1929   Electricity and x-ray equipment installed at Dohnavur, much to the wonder and amazement of the children.

1931   Amy slips and falls into a pit at Kalakadu, and begins 21 years of invalidity. In this period she pens 13 books, which are used by God both nationally and internationally.

1936   Amy's colleague, Arulai, dies.

1942   Measures are taken at Dohnavur for an expected Japanese invasion, which did not materialise.

1947   India gains independence from Britain, and the new flag of India is raised at Dohnavur.

1948   The dedication of girl-babies to Hindu temples is made illegal in the Tamil Nadu by the Madras Legislative Assembly.

1951   Amy dies.

1952   The Dohnavur Fellowship family numbers over nine hundred.

1954   The dedication of girl-babies to Hindu temples is made illegal for the whole of India by the Central Government of India in Delhi.